# Praise for *Leaving to Learn*

"Elliot Washor and Charles Mojkowski rightly identify student disengagement as the central cause of our nation's dropout crisis. Their solution—'leaving to learn'—connects education to the real world of life and work, creating highly engaged learners in the process. Their strategy—redesigning schools in fund understandable by this vivid and comp

—Linda Darling-Hammond, Cha
     Education, Stanford University

"*Leaving to Learn* puts forth a provocative and powerful argument: A significant number of capable young learners are dropping out of high school not because they can't meet their schools' expectations, but because schools don't meet theirs. The authors have worked with these young people and have some exciting insights to share about student engagement and intrinsic motivation. If you're concerned about the dropout problem, you owe it to the young people in your life to pick up this book."

—Daniel H. Pink, author of *Drive* and *A Whole New Mind*

"Washor and Mojkowski make a vital contribution to reinventing high schools for the 21st century in this important book. They understand, far better than most, how critical it is to engage and motivate students—to give them a reason to want to stay in school and to learn. This book is a must-read for anyone who truly wants to 'leave no child behind.'"

—Tony Wagner, author of *Creating Innovators* and *The Global Achievement Gap*

"This book is for anyone who wants to understand how schools can ignite the passions and interests of all children and help them make a difference in their world. Supporting learning out in the world is the key to unleashing their potential and to learning who they are and what they want to become."

—Suzy Amis Cameron, founder, board chair, MUSE School California

"School isn't something that kids are trying to do. Rather, they want to succeed at important things. Elliot Washor and Charles Mojkowski show the remarkable transformations in schools and their students when this becomes their focus."

—Clayton Christensen, Harvard business professor and author of *Disrupting Class: How Disruptive Innovation Will Change the Way the World Learns* and *How Will You Measure Your Life?*

"I applaud Elliot and Charles for their passion in serving students, impacting positive change, and ensuring we truly think about the education of our nation and beyond. This excellent book resets expectations and reengages us in the core of leadership in learning!"

—Stedman Graham, educator, entrepreneur, and author of *Identity: Your Pathway to Success*

"The authors get inside young people's heads and hearts in order to understand why and how they disengage from learning and often drop out. It's deeper than you think, the authors say, and they are right. Their solution is spot on—start with students' interests to break the cycle of failure. Here's hoping schools will listen."

—Pedro Noguera, Peter L. Agnew Professor of Education, New York University

# LEAVING

## TO LEARN

# ELLIOT WASHOR
# CHARLES MOJKOWSKI

# LEAVING TO LEARN

### HOW OUT-OF-SCHOOL LEARNING
### INCREASES STUDENT ENGAGEMENT
### AND REDUCES DROPOUT RATES

**HEINEMANN**
PORTSMOUTH, NH

**Heinemann**
361 Hanover Street
Portsmouth, NH 03801–3912
www.heinemann.com

*Offices and agents throughout the world*

The authors and publisher wish to thank those who have generously given permission to reprint borrowed material:

"Musée des Beaux Arts" from *Collected Poems of W. H. Auden* by W. H. Auden. Copyright © 1940 and renewed 1968 by W. H. Auden. Reprinted by permission of Random House, Inc., and Curtis Brown, Ltd. Any third-party use of this material, outside of this publication, is prohibited.

*Acknowledgments for borrowed material continue on p. xxx.*

**Library of Congress Cataloging-in-Publication Data**
Washor, Elliot.
    Leaving to learn : how out-of-school learning increases student engagement and reduces dropout rates / Elliot Washor and Charles Mojkowski.
        pages   cm
    Includes bibliographical references.
    ISBN-13: 978-0-325-04604-4
    1. Education, Secondary—United States.   2. Experiential learning—United States. 3. Student activities—United States. 4. Career education—United States. 5. Dropouts—United States—Prevention.   I. Mojkowski, Charles.   II. Title.
LA222.W34 2013
373.73—dc23                                                           2012048171

*Editor:* Holly Kim Price
*Development editor:* Alan Huisman
*Production:* Vicki Kasabian
*Interior and cover designs:* Lisa A. Fowler
*Typesetter:* Eric Rosenbloom, Kirby Mountain Composition
*Manufacturing:* Steve Bernier

Printed in the United States of America on acid-free paper

17  16  15  14  13  VP  1  2  3  4  5

## ELLIOT

*To my wife, Darlene, and my children,*
*Michael and Nathan,*
*for their love and support.*
*To all the students and staff in the Big Picture Learning*
*network who make leaving to learn a reality,*
*and to my childhood friends where I learned about*
*leaving to learn.*


## CHARLES

*To my wife, Corinne, and my children, Ellen and Mark,*
*for their love and inspiration.*
*To Lauren, my granddaughter,*
*that she may find delight in learning.*

# CONTENTS

FOREWORD BY SIR KEN ROBINSON   *xi*

PREFACE   *xv*

ACKNOWLEDGMENTS   *xxi*

INTRODUCTION   *xxiii*

## UNDERSTANDING DISENGAGEMENT   *1*

**1   Why Young People Disengage from School:
It's Deeper Than You Think**   *3*

The Big Four   *5*

The Deeper Four   *11*

**2   High Hopes: Students' Expectations**   *22*

Relationships   *24*

Relevance   *25*

Authenticity   *27*

Application   *29*

Choice   *30*

Challenge   *31*

Play   *32*

Practice   *34*

Time   *35*

Timing   *36*

Reasonable Questions All   *37*

**3   Leaning Toward Leaving: How Young People Disengage from
Their Schools**   *39*

"You've Changed"   *41*

Where Did the Love Go?   *43*

"It's Time to Say Goodbye"   *46*

Rethinking the Relationship   *48*

## ENGAGING STUDENTS IN PRODUCTIVE LEARNING   *51*

**4   What Constitutes Success?**   *53*

**5**    **What Is Important to Learn to Achieve Success?**   *57*

     An Uncommon Core   *57*

     No Head for Creativity   *59*

     All and Nothing   *61*

     Handmade Standards   *63*

     Approaching Standards   *65*

**6**    **How Should Schools Help Students Learn Productively?**   *70*

     Learning in the Funnel   *71*

     Productive Projects   *75*

     How Do We Know What's Been Learned?   *79*

     New Wine in New Bottles   *81*

## LEAVING TO LEARN   *85*

**7**    **Ways to Leave for Learning**   *87*

     Leaving-to-Learn Opportunities   *89*

     Come-Back Programs   *105*

**8**    **Supporting Leaving to Learn**   *108*

     The Basic Tools   *108*

     Beyond the Basic Tools   *110*

     Creating Alternative Learning Environments   *114*

## STUDENTS' EXPECTATIONS: THE NEW IMPERATIVES   *117*

**9**    **What Have We Learned?**   *119*

     So What?   *123*

     Who Can Help?   *126*

**10**    **What in the World Are We Coming To?**   *128*

     Act on "The Deeper Four" by Addressing Students' Expectations   *128*

     Focus on Productive Learning   *129*

     Adopt New Imperatives   *129*

     Conduct Research and Development   *131*

     Take on New Challenges   *131*

     Establish New Relationships   *133*

     Find New Ways of Innovating   *134*

WORKS CITED   *139*

ABOUT THE AUTHORS   *151*

*Leaving to Learn* is an inspiring and important book. It identifies many of the real issues that lie at the heart of the current crisis in education, and it says in very practical terms what should be done to remedy them.

In the United States, about one-third of students do not graduate from high school. Somewhere between the ninth and twelfth grades, they decide to walk away and leave it all behind them. In some communities, the rate is much higher. Some young people do reconnect with education in other ways, through taking the GED, for example, or through home schooling or by attending community college. Many do not. The personal, economic, and social costs are almost incalculable.

While many schools are hemorrhaging students, correctional systems across the country are filling up faster than ever. One in thirty-one adult Americans is now in the correctional system—the highest rate on earth. It would be wrong to say that students who pull out of school inevitably end up in jail. Of course they don't. What *is* true is that many of those in the correctional system did not do well in school or did drop out. In a tragic reversal of public priorities, many states are now cutting budgets for education while increasing them for the correctional system.

And yet, improving education and tackling the dropout rate, in particular, are among the nation's top priorities. Billions of dollars are spent on education every year; there are endless initiatives and countless debates on raising standards and improving results. Even so, the problems of disaffection and disengagement roll on relentlessly, and the dropout rate continues to haunt and perplex politicians on both sides. Significantly, the achievements of those who do stay in school have not improved either, despite the blizzard of legislation and special measures to "fix" education.

The truth is that most policies are tackling the problems of education from entirely the wrong perspective. Elliot Washor and Charles Mojkowski agree, and their Big Picture Schools demonstrate the principles and methods on which the real solutions to the crisis in education should be based. Let me point to three of them.

First, education is always and inevitably personal. All students have their own reasons for staying in, or for pulling out of, school. Like you and me they are living, breathing individuals with their own hopes, motivations, challenges, aptitudes, and drives. The current system is failing so many of them because it is impersonal and standardized. The future lies in forms of education that are customized to the needs and motivations of the people in it. This is why this book is focused on understanding *learners.*

Second, education is about *learning.* It can be improved only through a deeper understanding of why and how people actually do learn. The current system is failing because it typically force-feeds students a dry diet of received information. The solution is to adopt forms of teaching that arouse students' appetites for learning. The best way to do that is to cultivate the powers of imagination and creativity that lie dormant in so many students and teachers alike. This is why this book has so much to say about the nature of learning.

Third, focusing on learners and learning has important implications for the culture of schools. The current system is failing because it is rooted in the industrial culture of mass production—the fixed lesson periods and ringing bells, the division of students into age groups and the curriculum into separate subjects, and the rigid barriers between school and the world outside. Schools do not have to be like this. These conventions are all vestiges of the origins of mass education in the industrial revolution. The solution is for administrators and principals to be much more flexible and creative in how they run their own schools. This is why this book has so much to say about alternative approaches to school culture and especially about partnerships with the wider community and the world of work.

Washor and Mojkowski describe a sophisticated approach in their own schools in which all students from ninth to twelfth grade spend time every week working in other settings, from hospitals to design offices to restaurants. This is the essential strategy of *Leaving to Learn.*

The arguments in *Leaving to Learn* are supported by wisdom and theory from many sources, but the case it presents is not theoretical. It is rooted in the long experience of successful practitioners who know that the approach they are commending works and that they can prove it.

Some say that we can't afford to personalize education to all students. The truth is that we can't afford not to. The price we pay for the failures of the current system is more than we can bear. To succeed as it has to, education must engage the curiosity, creativity, aptitudes, and passions of every student. *Leaving to Learn* has vital lessons for all of us on how to do exactly that.

Sir Ken Robinson

*The face of the water, in time, became a wonderful book. . . .*
*And it was not a book to be read once and thrown aside,*
*for it had a new story to tell every day.*

—MARK TWAIN, *LIFE ON THE MISSISSIPPI*

The inspiration for this book came as we watched a Public Broadcasting Service (PBS) special on the 2008 and 2009 ceremonies awarding the Mark Twain Prize for American Humor at the Kennedy Performance Center, in Washington, DC. Created by the Kennedy Center, the prize recognizes humorists who have had an impact on American society in ways similar to those of nineteenth-century author and humorist Mark Twain (a.k.a. Samuel Clemens).

The awards ceremony is a decidedly highbrow affair for often lowbrow humor and humorists. The first recipient, in 1998, was the late Richard Pryor. Born in Peoria, Illinois, Pryor was expelled from school at fourteen and joined the U.S. Army but spent a good bit of his tour of duty in an army prison (Als 1999). The late George Carlin, comedian and actor, received the award in 2008. Carlin spent only three semesters at a Manhattan high school and briefly attended another in Harlem, dropping out in the tenth grade. While moonlighting as a disc jockey for a local radio station, he earned his high school equivalency diploma (Carlin and Hendra 2009). Comedian and writer Bill Cosby was honored in 2009. Cosby failed tenth grade and chose to apprentice at a shoe repair shop rather than repeat the year (Smith 1997). He joined the U.S. Navy and passed his high school equivalency exam while enlisted (Adler 1986). Cosby later returned to school, earned advanced degrees throughout his life, became an accomplished educator, and, as a major part of his life's work, used his talents to support educational opportunity (Maxwell 2010).

Watching the PBS program, we thought about how Pryor, Cosby, and Carlin, through their insightful and wry observations, made us laugh at ourselves and think differently about our society and have now received a national honor for their performances and writing. Not bad for three high school dropouts. Then again, who better than three castaways to become, true to Twain's legacy, social critics and contributors to a better society? Like Twain, they used humor to illuminate our follies and foibles, even our misdeeds.

As you might expect, Twain was also a dropout. His formal education ended when he was twelve years old, when he became a printer's apprentice and editorial assistant for his brother's newspaper. He then chose not school but the Mississippi as the classroom in which he learned to be a river pilot (Paine 1916). In his later years, school was definitely on his mind, however ("I never let my schooling interfere with my education" is a famous quip [Ayres 1987]), and it was a source of humor in his early novels. Twain was awarded a Doctor of Letters from Oxford University in 1907, finally obtaining that elusive degree (*New York Times* 1907).

We asked ourselves whether there were other Twain prize recipients who dropped out of high school or college. Research revealed that Carl Reiner, Jonathan Winters, and Whoopi Goldberg were high school dropouts. Steve Martin, Lily Tomlin, and Neil Simon were college dropouts (The John F. Kennedy Center 2011). Lily Tomlin (the 2003 awardee) entered Detroit's Wayne State University as a premed student because she wanted to be a doctor. But what she really wanted "was to have autonomy. In those years—remember, this is fifty years ago—you either had to be exceptional or be married. I never wanted to be depen - dent on anybody, and I was darn good in science." In her spare time she acted in school plays. After dropping out of Wayne State, she moved to New York and appeared in a variety of cabaret shows before she got her big break on the sketch-comedy television show, *Rowan & Martin's Laugh-In* (*Time* magazine 1977).

You might argue that Mark Twain, in the late 1800s, could do quite well without a high school diploma—many did back then—but times are very different now. Or you might contend that these dropouts are humorists and entertainers who did not need to learn Boyle's law or the Pythagorean theorem. Beyond encouraging them as class clowns, what could their schools have done to prepare them for their careers?

Even in these very different times, many famous people in all walks of life, of whatever race, class, or gender, have done very well without obtaining a high school diploma. Many other famous people never obtained a college degree, currently considered the green card for a successful career. Beyond the glare of celebrity are many more who left school and found success in widely disparate careers. These high achievers did most of their learning outside school (Coster 2010, Drell 2011).

American business magnate and philanthropist Bill Gates dropped out of Harvard University. He said it was a hard but necessary decision if he was to launch what would lead to Microsoft (The Gates Notes 2010). Marc Ecko, the founder and chief creative officer of Ecko Unlimited, left the Rutgers School of Pharmacy to pursue a career in clothing design. Today, Marc Ecko Enterprises, based in New York City, is a billion-dollar group of fashion, media, entertainment, and lifestyle companies (Marc Ecko Enterprises 2008).

American jazz saxophone player Stan Getz received straight As in school and was very proud of being near the top of his class in sixth grade, even as he played the sax nearly eight hours a day. He dropped out of high school despite being accepted into New York's All-City High School Orchestra and received free private tutoring from the New York Philharmonic's Simon Kovar, a bassoon player. The school system's truancy officers sent Getz back to the classroom, but he became a ward of bandleader Jack Teagarden, escaped their clutches, and never returned (Gelly 2002).

We could go on, but we've made our point. Many successful people left school without a high school or college diploma, and few from our list—Bill Cosby is an exception—ever returned. They dropped out to find better opportunities to develop their talents; without the learning they acquired outside school, it is unlikely they would have achieved to the degree they did. Ironically, many successful-in-life dropouts later receive honorary degrees but continue to feel inadequate without that high school diploma or college degree. Society frowns on and stigmatizes those who leave or never formally graduate. They really do miss something by leaving.

Ah, you might say, of course the people you mention had to leave to learn. Look at the drive they had! But isn't that 20/20 hindsight? Aren't you influenced by what you know now about these billionaire business moguls or talented artists and scientists? Would you have recognized their potential when they were still in school? Perhaps not. And how many talented students are today's schools failing to recognize among the nearly seven thousand who drop out every day?

Of course, few who drop out end up reaping outsized rewards. Many do poorly. Most who leave permanently to do their own thing don't do it well and struggle for many years or their entire lives. This is why educators say, "Just stay in school." What would you advise students who are considering leaving school to pursue some interest or are just bored silly—stay in school and soldier on? If they stay in school, will they have as much success? More? Different?

Staying the course is not a satisfying answer unless it is accompanied by a deeper understanding of what drives young people to leave school. We would like to ask successful dropouts: "If your teachers had asked you to bring your out-of-school interests into school and used them to engage you and shape your in-school learning, would you have stayed?" We think they would answer yes, particularly if that learning and work received recognition and academic credit. This is the essence of our insight and inspiration: how can we create schools that learners never want to drop out of, because there they are encouraged to learn by way of their out-of-school interests, learning that is blended with the learning they do in school?

Most education reform and redesign initiatives are not making a significant difference in the near-term and long-term prospects of many of the young people who attend school. We need, therefore, to approach the challenges more fundamentally. We need, as someone has said about the U.S. economy, "architectural change," change that will reduce the current dropout rate in urban high schools by 50 percent or more. Equally important, schools need to address the needs of the large number of young people who are "leaning toward leaving," remaining in their seats but dropping out in their heads.

Gary Hamel, a business advisor to organizations throughout the world, has written, "Strategy is revolution; everything else is tactics" (Hamel 1996). We have a bold strategy for revitalizing schools and for graduating and preparing young people for success in their future learning and work. This "leaving to learn" strategy is driven by our image of that future. Our goal is not merely to graduate every student but to prepare graduates who are uncommonly ready for success in their workplaces, their families, and their communities.

> OUR GOAL IS NOT MERELY TO GRADUATE EVERY STUDENT BUT TO PREPARE GRADUATES WHO ARE UNCOMMONLY READY FOR SUCCESS IN THEIR WORKPLACES, THEIR FAMILIES, AND THEIR COMMUNITIES.

What if there were lots of places where students with similar interests could form learning communities to learn more, both within and beyond those interests, from experts and peers? What if the school embraced an extended world of learning resources that appealed to and engaged young people in learning? What if there were ways to provide and give credit for learning wherever and whenever it occurred? What if the solution to preventing students from dropping out is to create deeply engaging learning opportunities and learning environments for *every* student?

Unlike many who write about improving schools, we work in schools that we have designed and continue to support—schools that respond positively to those "what ifs." Big Picture Learning schools are unconventional because we take an unconventional view of how schools might provide learning opportunities and environments that maximize learning for every single student. Much of our practice deliberately runs counter to accepted understanding about what constitutes success and how every student might achieve it. Core design components include personalized learning plans that start with students' interests and needs, learning through projects, learning in the real world, performance assessments, family engagement, and technology applications that support all aspects of the school and curriculum.

We are practitioner researchers; we pay close attention to research about how people learn in schools and in the real world. We are avid users of formal educational research but skeptical of it as well, primarily because of its considerable variation in quality and utility. We pay particular attention to the research on motivation and creativity. We challenge our own practice, principally by observing how young people use schools and the ways they interact with their teachers. Learning and improving are built into the culture of our Big Picture Learning schools, which is why many of them are second and third generation.

We draw much of our inspiration from watching the ways people think, learn, and perform in their occupations and in pursuing their interests and hobbies. We talk with many people in different walks of life: creative artists, scientists, tradesmen, magicians, doctors, engineers, lawyers, and tinkerers. How do they learn in their profession, trade, or craft? How do they learn by tinkering? By do-it-yourself projects? We observe the ways that people, especially young people, go about learning "when the teacher's not watching."

Lord John Reith, the first director-general of the British Broadcasting Company, once observed, "There are some people whom it is one's duty to offend!" (Ramachandran 2004). As we comment on what passes for innovation in the prevailing zeitgeist regarding school reform, we will undoubtedly offend some people. It cannot be otherwise. Our schools have become weapons of mass disengagement. Any serious effort at reforming them will necessarily entail a fundamental redesign, and ours is exactly that.

The world outside school has many stories to tell our young people and provides a powerful setting and context for their learning. Schools need to find a way to harness that resource. This book shows the way.

# ACKNOWLEDGMENTS

This book is a long time coming. It could've been—no, it nearly was—more than 500 pages. We hope that we have succeeded in distilling from all of our learning what is most useful for our readers. Working as practitioners, researchers, and change agent provocateurs provides us with invaluable perspectives, but it also weighs heavily on our time to reflect and write.

Many people have inspired and informed our work and specifically this book. We extend deep appreciation to the hundreds of students we have observed and talked with over the years. We have learned much from their stories. We are grateful to the families and mentors who have supported our students in their out-of-school learning.

Scores of principals and teachers in our Big Picture Learning schools provided us with examples of their work. Big Picture Learning staff members, past and present, have contributed to our learning journey. And, outside our own network, numerous colleagues have helped to improve the practices we write about here.

Dennis Littky, Big Picture Learning's cofounder and codirector, has been a decades-long codreamer and codesigner.

Several colleagues reviewed drafts of our work and provided insights and recommendations that have, we believe, improved our message. We give special thanks to Robert Pearlman, Sam Seidel, Talmira Hill, Sir Ken Robinson, and David Abel. We hope that we have done justice to their labors on our behalf.

Special thanks to Ellen Mojkowski for her unfailing research and organization skills and to Mark Mojkowski for the scores of conversations that have helped us to hone so many of our messages. Both gave extraordinary attention to this project, providing their dad with a special thrill to have them contributing so much to his work. Thanks as well to Lynda

Armstrong at Big Picture Learning for her attention to the list of myriad details that never seemed to diminish.

Holly Kim Price, Alan Huisman, and the Heinemann publishing staff provided good counsel and support from the very inception of this project right through to the approved galleys. They understood our message and helped us to communicate it.

To all of these individuals, thank you. We doubt that we have realized fully the expectations you had for us, but we are ever so thankful for your insights and advice.

Early in his presidency, President Obama (2009) stated that "dropping out of high school is no longer an option" (para. 66), signaling his intention to ensure that all young people obtain a high school diploma so they can earn higher wages, contribute to society, and lead fulfilling lives. Unfortunately, however, many youth *do* consider dropping out a viable option. And they don't just drop out of school; they drop out of productive learning and come to see themselves as failures. Nearly four years later, in January 2012, little progress having been achieved, the president called yet again for a response to the dropout crisis (The White House and Obama 2012).

His continuing concern is not misplaced. The nation's graduation rate for 2009 was 75.5 percent (Balfanz, Bridgeland, Bruce, and Hornig Fox 2012). More than one million students fall through the cracks in the high school pipeline every year (Balfanz et al. 2012), and nearly five million eighteen- to-twenty-four-year-olds lack a high school diploma (Princiotta and Reyna 2009). Approximately forty million Americans older than sixteen have not finished high school (Gewertz 2011). Among industrialized democracies, the United States ranks twentieth out of twenty-eight in the proportion of young people who finish high school (Princiotta and Reyna 2009). And those nongraduates are disproportionately members of historically disadvantaged minority groups (Balfanz et al. 2012).

These statistics are disturbing, and their persistence suggests intractability. Despite our schools' best efforts—and enormous increases in funding—the percentage of young people who leave high school without a diploma has hardly changed.

Alma Powell, Chair of America's Promise Alliance, illuminates the dimensions of the tragedy:

> If 7,000 children went missing today in this country, there's no doubt about what our response would be. Our communities would mobilize

all the resources at their disposal to get them back. The story would
dominate the media. There would be urgent investigations and new
policies to prevent it from happening again. Yet in a very real way, we
*are* losing 7,000 children—not just today but every day that school is
in session. They are dropping out, and most will not come back.
(Powell 2008)

Unfortunately, Mrs. Powell's illustration does not include an estimate
of the even larger number of students who disengage from learning at
some point during their high school or college experience but never actually drop out. We don't know about their talents or their post–high school
trajectories. Many students—in college as well as in high school—who
persist through graduation would love to leave to learn but don't know
how to do that learning outside school and connect it to school for academic and graduation credit.

Perhaps the dropout rate could be lowered if, as President Obama
suggested in his January 2012 State of the Union Address (The White
House and Obama 2012), Congress just passed a law against it. We see that
as counterproductive. To improve the education students receive so that
they don't want to drop out requires understanding why young people
leave school without obtaining a diploma. A 2010 synthesis of the dropout
research, *Achieving Graduation for All: A Governor's Guide to Dropout Prevention and Recovery* (Princiotta and Reyna 2009) (a report we contributed to), identified four major reasons young people leave school
without a diploma: academic failure, behavioral problems, life events,
and disinterest.

These four factors—we call them "the big four"—explain much
about the motivations for dropping out. Lifting the cover and looking a bit
closer, however, reveals that it's much deeper than the big four. Based on
our years of observing students in our own schools and listening to their
stories, we have identified four additional factors, "the deeper four," that
reveal even more about young people's perspectives: not fitting in; not
mattering; overlooked talents and interests; and restrictions.

Not only are the reasons for dropping out deeper than we think,
dropping out is in large part a consequence of a more widespread prob-

lem—the disengagement of students from their schools and from productive learning. Like the Russian *matryoshka* doll, the dropout crisis is nested within disengagement, thus motivating and requiring the dual focus of this book. The deeper four explain not only the large number of dropouts from our schools but also the even larger number of disengaged students who stay in school but drop out psychologically.

We hear often of the "high expectations" schools must have of and for their students, yet we seldom hear of the expectations students have of their schools. Students' expectations constitute the new "rules of engagement" in the relationship that young people want with their schools. Their expectations, framed as questions, are:

WE HEAR OFTEN OF THE "HIGH EXPECTATIONS" SCHOOLS MUST HAVE OF AND FOR THEIR STUDENTS, YET WE SELDOM HEAR OF THE EXPECTATIONS STUDENTS HAVE OF THEIR SCHOOLS.

**Relationships:** *Do my teachers and others who might serve as my teachers know about me and my interests and talents?*

**Relevance:** *Do I find what the school is teaching relevant to my interests?*

**Authenticity:** *Is the learning and work I do regarded as significant outside school by my communities of practice and by experts, family, and employers?*

**Application:** *Do I have opportunities to apply what I am learning in real-world settings and contexts?*

**Choice:** *Do I have real choices about what, when, and how I will learn and demonstrate my competence?*

**Challenge:** *Do I feel appropriately challenged in my learning and work?*

**Play:** *Do I have opportunities to explore—and to make mistakes and learn from them—without being branded as a failure?*

**Practice:** *Do I have opportunities to engage in deep and sustained practice of those skills I need to learn?*

**Time:** *Do I have sufficient time to learn at my own pace?*

**Timing:** *Can I pursue my learning out of the standard sequence?*

These are reasonable expectations, and they make clear that the real plague we're suffering is extraordinarily high levels of student disengagement and that dropping out is the ultimate consequence of that disengagement. Forcing a disengaged student to stay in school—whether by social pressure or by government edict—is as severe an indication of the failure of our educational system as a dropout is.

Crafting effective solutions involves a thorough understanding of the deteriorating relationship between young people and their schools—*how* as well as *why* students disengage. Increasing engagement and thereby reducing the number of dropouts requires that schools aggressively address student expectations, actively soliciting students' responses to these questions (much the way a Fortune 500 company might survey its most valuable customers) and welcoming the opportunity to reconstitute and revitalize the relationship they have with their students and focus that relationship on productive learning.

Inspired by Seymour Sarason's definition (in his 2004 book, *And What Do YOU Mean by Learning?*) (Sarason 2004) of productive learning as learning that "engenders and reinforces wanting to learn more" (x), we describe productive learning as denoting rigorous student work that focuses on demonstrations of competence and leads students to seek higher levels of accomplishment through craftsmanship, mastery, and artistry. Three perennial questions need to be addressed related to productive learning:

1.  What constitutes success?
2.  What is important to learn to achieve success?
3.  How should schools help students learn productively?

Although our answers to these questions are neither definitive nor unchanging, we see productive learning as applied in three important life roles: the workplace, the family, and the community.

Traditional instructional processes and assessments cannot bring all students to competence, much less craftsmanship and mastery. To keep students in school and engaged as productive learners through to graduation, schools must provide many experiences in which all students do some of their learning outside school. All students need to *leave* school—frequently, regularly, and, of course, *temporarily*—to stay in school and persist in their learning. To accomplish this, schools must take down the walls that separate the learning that students do, and could do, in school from the learning they do, and could do, outside. The learning in both settings and contexts must be seamlessly integrated.

ALL STUDENTS NEED TO LEAVE SCHOOL—FREQUENTLY, REGULARLY, AND, OF COURSE, TEMPORARILY—TO STAY IN SCHOOL AND PERSIST IN THEIR LEARNING.

We call such a program "leaving to learn."

If the notion of leaving school in order to learn appears counterintuitive, that's all right. It is fair to ask: How will students learn anything if they are not in school? To answer this question we need to push back the boundaries of what we take for granted about learners, learning, and schools. We see leaving to learn as quite normal; in Big Picture Learning schools nearly all our students do a considerable amount of their learning outside school. It's natural for us to think about ways in which students can leave our schools—and all schools—to learn and bring that learning back into school.

Leaving-to-learn opportunities include internships, travel, community service, work, entrepreneurial ventures, and gap years. Many schools provide a few of these opportunities, but it is rare to find whole-school leaving-to-learn programs that are open to all students in all grades, are an integral part of students' learning plans, and are awarded academic and graduation credit. By employing such programs, schools can deliver on students' expectations and help them learn at "the edge of their competence." It's not just about getting students out early and often, but about what they do when they get out and how they bring their learning and accomplishments back to school. Drawing on the world outside school to identify the structures and cultures required to make leaving-to-learn work effectively, we see new roles for educators as talent spotters, travel agents, brokers, and personal trainers and coaches.

Leaving-to-learn programs also help schools address another population of young people—those who have recently dropped out and wish to drop back in. These "come back" programs also help the school reach out into the community (physically and virtually) to bring learning resources to young people in out-of-school settings.

The new policies and protocols that support leaving-to-learn systems need the support of parents, employers, and the community. All those who serve young people, whether through their policies, programs, or practices, need to embrace truly significant innovations, quite unlike the current timid, toe-in-the-water initiatives that have required the president to reiterate his plea for education reform.

Few of our Big Picture Learning students drop out, even though the overwhelming majority of them have encountered some or all of the big-four reasons for doing so. Why do they stay? For many reasons, but principal among them is that our schools pay close attention to the deeper four and address student expectations. Much of each student's highly motivational and engaging learning takes place outside school and is recognized as important and eligible for academic credit.

Leaving to learn is not a theory but a carefully honed system that continues to evolve in a hundred schools around the globe. We are also helping many non–Big Picture Learning schools adapt the system for their students. These questions guide our narrative:

- What do young people want from their schools?
- How can leaving-to-learn programs significantly increase the number of young people who stay in school through graduation, deeply engaged in productive learning?
- What are the critical design features and components of leaving-to-learn and come-back programs?
- What changes will educators need to make in their schools to support leaving-to-learn and come-back programs?

Most young people find school hard to use. Indeed, many young people find school a *negative* learning environment. Not only do schools fail to help students become competent in important life skills, they provide a warped image of learning as something that takes place only in schools, segregated from the real world, organized by disciplines and school bells, and assessed by multiple-choice, paper-and-pencil tests. Schools have scores of written and unwritten rules that stifle young people's innate drive for learning and restrict their choices about at what they want to excel, when to practice, from whom to learn, and how to learn. It is no wonder that so many creative and entrepreneurial youth disengage from productive learning. They recognize that staying in the schools we offer them constitutes dropping out from the real world.

Schools largely ignore the abundant research on learners and learning, particularly that dealing with motivation, engagement, and creativity. Attention—giving it to each young person in exchange for his or hers—is the name of the game that schools refuse to play. Schools' attention deficit disorder is a threat to their success. Sir Ken Robinson (2001) and other authorities on creativity and invention remind us of the dire consequences of ignoring and failing to develop the innate creativity and inventiveness of our young learners.

To get to something really different and better, educators need to think about learners and learning differently. They need to question their taken-for-granted assumptions, forget what they know about schools, reason with a beginner's mind, and see possibilities with new eyes—particularly through the eyes of one young learner at a time.

If you are not ready to think and act so differently, it might be best to look elsewhere for your school reform design. But relinquish any thoughts of addressing the deeper four and delivering on student expectations, and resign yourself to living with high dropout rates and levels of disengagement. John Masters, an Australian oilman, once said:

> You have to recognize that every "out-front" maneuver is going to be lonely. But if you feel entirely comfortable, then you're not far enough ahead to do any good. That warm sense of everything going well is usually the body temperature at the center of the herd. Only if you're far enough ahead to be at risk do you have a chance for large rewards. (Biggs 2006, 120)

The real risk, therefore, is to do nothing. And, for us, and we hope for you, that is not an option.

*Credit lines continued from copyright page:*

The Knowledge Funnel on page 71 was published previously on edutopia's blog on April 5, 2011. Available at www.edutopia.org/blog/knowledge-funnel-learning-elliot-washor-charles-mojkowski.

# Understanding Disengagement

The intractable and persistent school dropout crisis has attracted lots of solutions, ranging from improved early identification systems to special programs and schools for students who are leaning toward dropping out, those halfway out the door, and those already gone who might wish to come back. In the first three chapters, we propose that these interventions may be more successful, or might not be needed at all, if schools broaden their focus to address the problem of student disengagement. This focus is guided by a deeper understanding of not only why and how students drop out of school but also why and how many more students become disengaged from productive learning.

We'll look at the abundant research on why students drop out but also identify additional factors drawn from our own experience that lead to a better sense of how schools might address those factors. We will also look at the notion of expectations from the students' perspective. Finally, we will attempt to get inside the heads—and hearts—of students to understand what the process of disengaging looks like to them.

Let's get started.

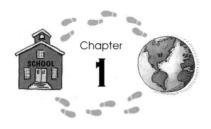

# WHY YOUNG PEOPLE DISENGAGE FROM SCHOOL

## IT'S DEEPER THAN YOU THINK

*School-days, I believe, are the unhappiest in the whole span of human existence. They are full of dull, unintelligible tasks, new and unpleasant ordinances, brutal violations of common sense and common decency.*

—HENRY LOUIS MENCKEN

Mencken's early twentieth-century dismissal of school was neither the first nor the last. In 1957, Chuck Berry wrote "Too Much Monkey Business," and his description of schools' everyday hassles, their sameness and boredom, and their unresponsiveness to students' objections both echoes and mirrors contemporary schools. A generation before Berry's lament, Jacques Cousteau had already learned that school was a place for boredom and restrictions. Despite being a sickly child, Cousteau loved to swim from a very young age. At ten years old, he was already trying to hold his breath underwater for as long as he could and used tubing to stay down longer. Cousteau also loved to take apart machines and put them back together. At eleven years old, he built a five-foot model marine crane and a battery-operated car. At school, Cousteau was bored and considered a poor student. Biographer Lesley DuTemple (2000) writes: "Machines were his only interest, he claimed. Machines did magical things! He wanted to drop all other subjects and study only machines" (14). But teachers refused this request. So Cousteau cut classes, broke things, and lied. He was expelled for breaking seventeen windows and claiming he wanted the windows to look as though cowboys had shot them out.

It would be unreasonable to expect Cousteau's teachers to recognize the future co-inventor of the aqualung and internationally renowned explorer and conservationist. Nevertheless, his teachers knew nothing of his interests and exploits outside of school—to see the world, to make movies, to swim.

A generation after Berry's complaint about schools, Canadian-born newscaster Peter Jennings was hosting his own radio show at age nine, yet struggled in school. He later reflected that it was out of "pure boredom" that he failed tenth grade and dropped out. "I loved sports. I loved girls," he said. "I loved comic books. And for reasons I don't understand, I was pretty lazy" (Darnton, Jennings, and Sherr 2008, 6). Jennings briefly attended Carleton University before dropping out. He also attended the University of Ottawa.

Jennings was brought up around reporters. His father was a pioneer in Canadian radio, often referred to as the Walter Cronkite or Edward R. Murrow of Canada. Peter's interests in radio and TV drove him. He wanted no part of school learning; he was too active and too inquisitive to sit still. So his traditional academic skills were subpar. His sister Sarah recalled, "It's quite true that when he came and took the first job, he lacked a really solid grounding that anyone who had gone through the American educational system would have, but he had the desire to learn, the desire to know, and he was not afraid to ask questions. . . . But from the point of view of his own interests, that's how he learned."

You might think that Jennings' schools would be ecstatic to have a student like this. Instead there was no place for his interests in the curriculum, so the world outside became his learning environment. From his relationships with adults he learned about the challenges of the real world. He realized that he needed more than school, and he was not going to deny himself those opportunities.

Similar stories of young people make the news from time to time. Sixteen-year-old Jessica Watson, from Australia, took seven months off to sail single-handedly around the world (Batty 2010). Jordan Romero climbed every continent's tallest peak before his fifteenth birthday (BBC News US & Canada 2011, Shimura 2010). Schools' failure to validate such capabilities and achievements defies common sense. How can students make history and not get credit for it, while students in school *do* receive credit for reading a story about that history? If we are perplexed by the rigidity of schools' expectations, aren't students even more so?

Dropout research identifies four big reasons many young people disengage from school, leave without a diploma, and rarely if ever return: academic failure, behavioral problems, life events, and disinterest. Our observations of students and schools indicate that beneath these big-four reasons (and often off the researchers' radar screens) are four deeper reasons: not fitting in, not mattering, overlooked talent and interests, and restrictions. While the big-four reasons drive policy, the deeper four provide insights into what many young people feel about their schools.

# THE BIG FOUR

Students who eventually drop out of high school exhibit strong warning signs, such as infrequent attendance, behavior infractions, and academic failure. In *Building a Grad Nation* (2011, 2012), Robert Balfanz and his colleagues report that these warning signs—the ABCs of dropping out— more accurately predict whether a student will drop out of high school than socioeconomic factors do and can be used to predict high school graduation as early as the start of middle school.

## ACADEMIC FAILURE

In *The Silent Epidemic* (2006), John Bridgeland, John Dilulio, and Karen Burke Morison report that about one-third of dropouts stated that fail-

ing academically was a major factor in their leaving school: they could not keep up, or they missed too many school days. Nearly half said they were not adequately prepared to start high school. About one-third were required to repeat a grade, and about one-third felt that it was unlikely that they could have met their schools' requirements even if they put in the effort.

Academic failure is pretty straightforward. Test scores, grades, and accrued course credits indicate that the student will not be able to graduate without spending more time repeating failed courses. But does academic failure, particularly as measured by traditional tests, necessarily mean failure to do academic work? We don't think so.

Schools monitor grades and Carnegie units (hours a student must be in a seat to receive credits) and inform students of their chances of graduation. Often, state and district tests also determine who will get a diploma.

Students do the calculations and decide to leave when the numbers don't add up and they see no way of catching up.

John Elder Robison is a self-taught electronics and restoration mastermind and owner of J E Robison Service, an independent automobile repair business specializing in Land Rover, Rolls Royce, and Bentley vehicles (Robison 2011a). In *Be Different*, Robison (2011b) reflects on his failure in several school courses:

> Measured against those tangible prospects, the idea of slogging through high school and then getting accepted at a college and doing it all again for four more years just seemed unreal. The first problem was the humiliation I'd face when every other tenth grader besides me became an eleventh grader. How many other kids flunked school? I wondered. I could not imagine three more years of high school. (61)

Robison, who has Asperger syndrome (high-functioning autism), dropped out of high school in the tenth grade. He did receive an honorary diploma in 2008 (when he was fifty-one) from the Monarch School of Houston (a school dedicated to individuals with neurological differences).

A Big Picture Learning student who also struggled with the culture and structure of her previous traditional high schools told us her story. Germaine explained:

> Of course, I am falling behind. Of course, my grades suffer. It's because I cannot get my head around the stuff they are teaching. I can learn, but not their stuff in their way. I understand that what they are teaching may get me ready for college, but I am not interested in that kind of college. I want to learn and work with my hands as well as my mind. I cannot stay just in my head. It's not what I want to do with my life.

These and similar stories (we have scores of them) reveal the nuances of and subtleties in "academic failure." Research and our own experience indicate that many young people, even those with passing grades, do not really understand the course content or the required curriculum. Yes, they pass the tests. But did they learn anything? The sad truth is not that a student gets an F because of limited understanding but that a student can get an A and yet understand little more. Many students who pass standard-ized tests, even high school graduation tests, are often deemed unready for college by the very colleges that have accepted them.

Of course, many dropouts have poor grades, but many of these stu-dents are capable of progressing academically if their schools would only engage them appropriately. This does not mean that they cannot learn but that they did not learn what, when, and how the school taught the cur-riculum. Often, these young people come to see themselves as poor learn-ers or not smart in the traditional school sense.

## BEHAVIOR

Students are removed or remove themselves from school because of seri-ous behavioral issues, including violence and threats of violence, drug use, high absenteeism, and disregard for school rules. About a quarter of high school dropouts, Richard Pryor among them, fall into this category. Behavioral issues often arise for other reasons as well, such as disinterest and boredom.

Some behavior cannot be tolerated. Violence and drug use are obvi-ous examples. Wildly disruptive behavior must be seen as wholly beyond schools' and teachers' abilities to address. That said, we have observed re-markable and immediate changes in behavior when students feel the school accommodates them by addressing the deeper four reasons for dropping out and students' expectations. Here's an illustration:

> Yesterday Elizabeth Lee and her advisor, Alex, presented to 200 people in Minneapolis/St. Paul at the state charter/small school conference. There was hardly a dry eye in the house after Elizabeth began by read-ing her college essay [on] how her Met experience changed her life. Three years before, on day one with us, Elizabeth came in screaming, cursing, and brawling. Who wouldn't be? She was moved from foster care placement to foster care placement and from school to school. The change in Elizabeth's presence over these years is transforma-tional. Alex told the audience her bravado was replaced by substance and empathy. He talked about the "hang in there" time it takes to work with each student. (Big Picture Learning 2004)

It is possible to reduce students' unacceptable behavior—even extreme problems like drug use and gang membership—by personalizing learning opportunities, engaging students in productive learning, and relaxing restrictions.

## LIFE EVENTS

The late Dr. Israel Gelfand, one of the most notable mathematicians of the twentieth century and himself a high school dropout out, told this story:

> During the Jewish pogrom massacres, in a Ukrainian shtetl, a few schools continued to function. After one of the pogroms, a biology teacher was lecturing on the life of insects. One Jewish boy was not paying attention. The teacher turned to him and asked, "Moshe, how many legs does a beetle have?"
>
> Moshe looked at the teacher with sorrow in his eyes, "I wish I had your problems, Professor!" (Gelfand and Gelfand 2009)

Gelfand was expelled from school for political reasons (perhaps a "push-out" rather than a dropout), but that didn't stop him from his love affair with math. He continued his studies through books and his visits to university libraries. Ahead of his time, he started correspondence schools in Russia so students with an interest in math could access mathematicians who would mentor, teach, and guide them. He knew from his own experiences that his failure to finish high school did not mean he was not academically smart.

Many dropouts describe personal reasons for leaving school. Bridgeland, Dilulio, and Morison (2006) state that about one-third reported they had to get a job and make money; a quarter said they became a parent; and about a fifth said they had to care for a family member. Many of these young people reported doing reasonably well in school and had a strong belief that they could have graduated if they had stayed in school. These students also were the most likely to say they would have worked harder if their schools had demanded more of them and provided the necessary support (read, met the students' expectations). Life issues are particularly challenging because most schools typically do not control the resources to address them, and the necessary links to appropriate agencies are difficult to establish and sustain.

Many young people we talked to told us that a combination of reasons prompted their decisions to leave. One student, for example, reported having a fight with his mother, feeling unsafe at school, and working sixty hours a week to support himself. The school counseled him away from college and into the Army. But, he said, "the Army is not who I am."

Life events caught up with John Elder Robison (2011b) as well:

> The world outside was full of opportunity. I was doing more and more work for local musicians, and I could probably join a band full-time. I could probably get work fixing cars, as a mechanic. There were other things I could do, too, like drive a truck or run farm machinery. I was already doing small jobs for people and getting paid.

Life events such as Robison's can be positive, but are nevertheless usually stressful, even when dropouts reported that their decision to leave was the right one. Sometimes dropping out addresses an immediate problem but not necessarily a long-term one.

## DISINTEREST

Bridgeland and his colleagues (2006) found that about half of dropouts reported being disinterested in what their schools had to offer. Disinterest is a major contributor to academic failure and behavioral problems. Young people feel that schoolwork is not relevant to where they are in their lives and in the world they experience outside school.

Does disinterest in how and what is being taught cause acting out? Does it cause academic failure? If students are interested and a teacher or adult engages them, does it make it easier to stay in school? Mihayli Csikszentmihalyi and Barbara Schneider (2000) have documented considerable disengagement even among students taking advanced placement courses. Daniel Pink (2009) feels that the carrot-and-stick industrial model of schooling plays heavily into the disengagement of students and the dropout crisis. Student motivation and engagement are essential to learning.

Most of the famous dropouts and students we've described above would certainly identify boredom and disinterest as major factors for leaving school. How could school compare with the opportunities they saw outside? These students were not necessarily disinterested in learning. Rather, they were interested in learning things the school did not address.

Imogene, a student in one of our schools in Australia, provides yet another perspective on disinterest: Her passion—and career goal—was graphic design. Initially her high school provided limited opportunity to address that interest. She struggled to find the motivation to come to school. The following year she transferred to a new Big Picture Learning program at her school and is now able to work on her skills and create a portfolio of work based on a fictional client. By working on something she is interested in, Imogene is at school regularly. She wants to be in school; she wants to devote the time to set goals and further her education. She says, "I want to be at school. . . . I am doing what I want to do."

Students are engaged in many things but not always the things that schools want them to be engaged in. They get tired of delaying the gratification obtained from doing the learning and work they wish to do. They want to move ahead with their own life plans. As James Cameron, renowned director of the films *Titanic* and *Avatar*, said, "I couldn't do what I needed to do in school. They told me that I needed what they were selling in order to succeed. I doubted they were right" (Cameron 2012).

The research supporting the big four—what we might call the obvious four—is sound and compelling. Typically, the "early warning systems" that some schools employ to identify potential dropouts are based on the big four, but these systems often are little more than simplistic algorithms that provide meager insight into the mysteries of student disengagement from their schools and from productive learning.

## THE DEEPER FOUR

Pedro Noguera (2004), urban sociologist and professor of education at New York University, observes:

> If we were more willing to listen and solicit their opinions, we might
> find ways to engage students more deeply in their own education.
> The students may not have the answers to the problems confronting
> high schools, but perhaps if we engage them in discussions about how
> to make school less alienating and more meaningful, together
> we  might find ways to move past superficial reforms and break the
> cycle of failure. (para. last)

For more than fifteen years, we have been listening to young people and observing how they relate to their schools. Their stories reveal another, deeper layer of more complex reasons beneath the big four.

## NOT MATTERING

In her acceptance speech for the 2005 Academy Award for Best Actress, Reese Witherspoon quoted June Carter Cash (whom she portrayed in the film *Walk the Line*) summing up her life's purpose: "I'm just trying to matter."

Mattering is how students see themselves as significant. Often this is influenced heavily by how others, including people in schools, see them.

Young people need to know that who they are, what they want to become, and what they are going through matters in school and in the greater community, and they need it affirmed by the school and by their teachers. Young learners ask themselves, *Does the school care about my interests or who I am?* Sadly, many students conclude that their schools do not.

Brené Brown, in *The Gifts of Imperfection* (2010), captures what young people—and more than a few adults—experience. The book's subtitle says it all: "Let go of who you think you're supposed to be and embrace who you are." Schools make it hard for young people to follow Brown's advice. As one of our students said of his former school: "They knew my weaknesses, but that is all they knew about me." And it's true: the bottom line for measuring learning in most schools is knowing what students *cannot* do, not what they *can*. And seldom are weaknesses viewed as insights into strengths.

A dramatic monologue performed by Ariel, a Big Picture Learning student from Camden, captures her failed efforts to matter in her former school:

*To all the educators who see the big picture.*
*13 schools, 8 grades, my education photograph started to fade.*
*And those snapshots or backdrops could explain my boredom.*
*These antique techniques they tried to teach me wasn't reaching me,*
*though my report card said I was passing.*
*And my teachers were walking contradictions.*
*They told me to follow my dreams.*
*But they retained my convictions as they signed their names only to my*
    *detention,*
*snapped their fingers in hopes to gain my attention,*
*shoved textbooks in my hands and gave tests in hopes that my retention*
    *would get them to a tenure track position.*
*They were training my millennial mind to the industrial revolution.*
*By my freshman year, I was crucified between standardized tests and*
    *report cards.*
*My want for knowledge was fading like a dull number 2 pencil.*
*I couldn't make a mark on the Scantron.*
*And we all know what happens when you don't fill that bubble.*
*My picture had no life, no focus, was broken.*
*My education was superficial.*

Our colleague, Frank Wilson, a neurologist and author of *The Hand: How Its Use Shapes the Brain, Language, and Human Culture* (1998), shared with us W. H. Auden's metaphor for the challenge of mattering found in *Landscape with the Fall of Icarus*, a painting done by Pieter Bruegel around 1558. The painting records the youthful Icarus falling into the sea as several adults ignore his failed attempt to fly near the sun. Auden (1938/n.d.) captures the essence of the painting in "Musée des Beaux Arts," a poem in which he focuses not on the hubris—or youthful exuberance—that motivated Icarus' quest to soar to great heights but rather on how the world ignored his plight:

*In Breughel's Icarus, for instance: how everything turns away*
*Quite leisurely from the disaster; the ploughman may*
*Have heard the splash, the forsaken cry,*

*But for him it was not an important failure; the sun shone*
*As it had to on the white legs disappearing into the green*
*Water, and the expensive delicate ship that must have seen*
*Something amazing, a boy falling out of the sky,*
*Had somewhere to get to and sailed calmly on.*

Both the painting and the poem communicate the disconnect between society and Icarus—he an outlier with aspirations a bit beyond his grasp, a mind of his own, and interests and passions that seem not to matter to others. They are reminders of the many ways schools ignore young people.

At one of the out-of-school youth symposia that Big Picture Learning conducted in 2010, one student spoke of that disregard: "My lack of credits and the fact that no one knew me [at his former high school] made it hard to go back. The school let students like me slide out the back door to keep their test scores up." Another lamented about his former high school: "I love to write short stories at home. But none of it counted for school. The size of the school was really intimidating, and I couldn't get any personal attention there. After getting left back, I had a huge disconnect."

Lynsea, a student at a Big Picture Learning school, is a kind of Icarus. A Native American with strong roots in her community and family, Lynsea struggled in a traditional high school that failed to look beyond her attention deficit issues to discover her considerable talents. A year after her transfer to a Big Picture Learning school, her advisor describes the transformation:

> She has been able to shine as the exceptional student that she is.
> Lynsea is in the accelerated math program and is a gifted writer and
> strong public speaker. Currently she interns with the Fire Chief with a
> focus on forensic science. She attends the weekly Forensic Science
> Lab at the University.

As Brené Brown maintains, letting go of who you think you're supposed to be and embracing who you are is important, but it is even more important to create yourself and get support from your school as you, in Nietzsche's words (2007), "become what you are."

Schools might contend that putting out-of-school interests aside and focusing on what the school has to offer is part of growing up. Students argue that their schools squander opportunities to engage them in learning by failing to know them. For schools to get the attention of their students, the schools must first give them theirs. Yet schools have their own attention deficit disorders.

## NOT FITTING IN

Young people need to find out who they are, and they need a sense of place as a way to do that. They need and want to fit into a community and connect to others who share their interests. So strong is this need that many young people take on personas that help them to fit in, in school, in their families, and in society. This is particularly true with respect to fitting in with a peer group.

Fitting in is the yin to mattering's yang. When young people find they do not matter in the school and cannot find a way to fit in, they look for other places to satisfy their need to learn and succeed.

We hear a lot about the mismatch between students and schools. Students ask, "Can I fit in even though I learn differently? Can I fit in even though I look different? Or sound different?" For some, it's the schedule. For others, it's the content. For still others, it's the pedagogy. Perhaps the fit is too tight or too loose. For Lynsea, the right fit provides an opportunity to wrap an academic curriculum around her Native American heritage. It's an opportunity to alter the pace and the timing of her learning to achieve productive learning.

Neurologist and author Oliver Sacks, in his *New Yorker* magazine piece titled "Brilliant Light" (1999), reported:

> I had been spoiled, in a sense, by my two uncles, and the freedom and spontaneity of my apprenticeship. Now, at school, I was forced to sit in classes, to take notes and exams, to use textbooks that were flat, impersonal, deadly. What had been fun, delight, when I did it in my own way became an aversion, an ordeal, when I had to do it to order. (72)

Undoubtedly, it takes considerable intellect and energy to start with students and gear content and related essential skills and understandings to their interests. But that is what students want and need. Instead, the schools require that all students address the same standards in the same way at the same time. We can think of few other democratic institutions that would require such regimentation to educate a citizenry, much less a globally competitive workforce.

## UNRECOGNIZED TALENTS AND INTERESTS

While few young people have the drive, luck, timing, and talents that would make them internationally famous, all students do have interests and talents that can help them be successful in their careers, families, and communities. We are not talking here only about being good in math or English but of developing interests and talents that go beyond the increasingly archaic subject matter of high schools. Schools are not talent spotters, however, and few teachers see themselves as talent scouts. Perhaps the coach or the art or music teacher plays this role, but it is a highly unusual one for the classroom teacher or principal to assume. And few schools have a structured process for doing so.

Here's a story about schools and talent we heard from a friend:

> When Vance was about twelve years old, his dad, Richie, did what all good dads do with their twelve-year-olds in Brooklyn: Richie took Vance to play pool in a pool hall. Richie had left school at fourteen and became one of the best pool players in New York City. Vance, as you might expect, was interested in pool and asked his dad to take him to the pool hall, so that he could show his father his pool skills. After Vance shot pool for a while, his dad told him, "You don't have any talent; you better stay in school."

Despite his limited schooling, Richie's advice to his son was most insightful. If a young person has a marketable talent, Richie reasoned, he should leave school and hone his talent in order to support himself and his family. Richie did not see schools as a place to develop talents. Fortunately, or unfortunately, on that day in the pool hall, Vance didn't display any talent that his father could see, so he stayed in school, but years later his father's wisdom was not lost on him. After graduating college he took an internship at a physiological lab to hone his talents, those the school could not see but the real world could. After a few years at the lab and armed with real-world experience and references, he was accepted into a graduate program and earned a Ph.D. in physiological psychology.

Regarding talent, psychologist Howard Gardner has observed:

> The time has come to redefine giftedness and broaden our notion of the spectrum of talents. The single most important contribution education can make to a child's development is to help him toward a field where his talents best suit him, where he will be satisfied and competent. We've completely lost sight of that. Instead we subject everyone to an education where, if you succeed, you will be best suited to be a college professor. And we evaluate everyone along the way according to whether they meet that narrow standard of success. We should spend less time ranking children and more time helping them identify their natural competencies and gifts, and cultivate those. There are hundreds and hundreds of ways to succeed, and many, many different abilities that will help you get there. (Goleman 1986, para. 6)

In the documentary *Les Paul—Chasing Sound!* Paul (2007), world-renowned guitarist and inventor of the solid body electric guitar and multitrack recording, describes his childhood:

> Radio was brand-new in those days, and I got hooked on it. It was the most exciting thing in the world (0:18:43–0:18:50). . . . So I would get on my bicycle and drive out and park right under the transmitter, and the engineer saw that I was very interested in electronics. So he said, tell you what, if you come out here every Sunday, I'll teach you. And so at the same time I was going to school I was also learning about electronics. (0:19:23–0:19:44)

He also explains how, in 1932, guitarist Joe Wolverton asked him to be partners. Paul's mother suggested he complete one more year of school so he could graduate. Seventeen-year-old Paul's response: "I don't care about algebra and who sank the *Titanic*. I says, nothing means nothing to me, just Joe" (0:20:01–0:20:08). So, this future National Inventors Hall of Fame inductee simply left school.

Paul, who performed regularly until his death in 2011 at 93, was in a car accident when he was a teenager and broke his right arm. When he was told he would not be able to play anymore, he showed the doctor how to set his arm in a way that would allow him to continue to strum—would that his school could have taken advantage of such a drive to learn.

Django Reinhardt, another world-famous guitarist without a high school diploma, burned his left hand in a fire when he was eighteen, rendering it permanently malformed. Undaunted, he adjusted his style and continued to play, thereby creating a totally new sound that influenced generations of players (Cole 2010). Talent will out, as they say, if only schools are willing to look beyond and beneath weaknesses to discover and develop strengths.

Consider also the story told by Ang Lee, 2005 Academy Award–winning director of the film *Brokeback Mountain* (Hollander 2007). Lee twice failed the college entrance exam in Taiwan, a country all about high academic achievement. He ended up going to a lowly regarded arts school where he learned filmmaking. No one in the school tried to find out about Lee's aspirations and interests.

Playwright and poet Langston Hughes (1940/1993), a major figure in the Harlem Renaissance Movement in the 1920s and 1930s, had a similar experience. His father would pay for his college only if he studied engineering at Columbia. So Hughes complied for the first year but then dropped out. He wrote of his sad experience at Columbia, where he skipped most classes to do his learning through reading, lectures, and other of New York's cultural resources. Only through a benefactor was he able to attend Lincoln University and complete a degree. By then, Hughes had already established his reputation.

Benjamin Bloom, in *Developing Talent in Young People* (1985), found that schools are not very good at spotting or developing talent. Bloom studied young people who excelled in the arts, sciences, sports, and games and found a typical pattern: (1) these young people had an interest and some talent they wanted to pursue; (2) a mentor of some sort told them and their parents early on they had some talent; (3) the young people made the decision to pursue their talents and, as they improved, they attracted better mentors and coaches. Lauren Sosniak, Bloom's researcher-colleague, sadly concluded, "Our current methods of instruction may be quite inappropriate for the long-term development of talent. We have a tendency, it seems, to emphasize momentary attentiveness, the acquisition of quickly acquired and simplistic skills, and immediate success" (Sosniak 1989, 288).

Young people are not always good at recognizing their own talents, and the certainty, rigidity, and inauthentic nature of school make it hard to discover and validate talents. Schools often engender doubts and insecurities about not being smart based solely on students' academic performance. Therefore, many young people look to discover and develop their talents and interests outside school.

## RESTRICTIONS

School restrictions come in many flavors, and students get a taste of them all. The inflexibility of the schedule, the lockstep scope and sequence, the regimentation, and the required readings are just a few of the restrictions that turn students off and impede productive learning.

Richard Epstein (2007), former editor-in-chief of *Psychology Today* and author of *Teen 2.0*, comments on his research:

> Surveys I have conducted show that teens in the U.S. are subjected to more than ten times as many restrictions as mainstream adults, twice as many restrictions as active-duty U.S. Marines, and even twice as many restrictions as incarcerated felons (59). . . . The truth is that [teens] are extraordinarily competent, even if they do not normally express that competence. . . . We need to replace the myth of the immature teen brain with a frank look at capable and savvy teens in history, at teens in other cultures and at the truly extraordinary potential of our own young people today. (63)

Schools are places of compliance, with restraints and restrictions built into the school organization and culture. The rationale is that young people need structure, and indeed they do, but the structure that schools impose is one that impedes productive learning and prevents students from learning how to create their own. Our conversations with students reveal that they are not against restrictions if they emanate from the requirements of authentic learning and work. Indeed, students will place enormous demands on themselves if they respect the learning.

Students are trying to establish what researchers call "locus of control." A student in our first graduating class reflected, "I dropped out because in my old school I had no say and no way to get say." The act of leaving school can be courageous, self-affirming, and life changing. Leaving is a powerful choice to exercise, and young people seldom make it lightly.

Restrictions placed on youth while they are in school prevent them from having the productive learning experiences they crave. Students don't have enough opportunities of their own choosing in the daily school routine to pursue significant and enduring learning and to be treated as the young adults they will soon become. Lacking such opportunities, many young people do not sit still; they disengage, either psychologically or physically.

In our work with schools that wish to adopt features and components of the Big Picture Learning school design, we have encountered many teachers and principals who feel a similar loss of control. Many of them leave the profession because the compliance requirements restrict their efforts to focus on their students' needs and to bring their own creativity and inventiveness to the challenges of helping all students engage in productive learning.


These eight reasons—the big four and the deeper four—and their combinations explain why young people leave school and do not return. They also account for why so many more students who remain in school through graduation are so disengaged from productive learning. These students sit in their seats and go through the motions, gaming the system. They have learned how to excel at the kind of learning traditional schools provide without necessarily becoming productive learners.

It is possible to view going to school as one of the oldest forms of dropping out. Schools, after all, were cloistered and monastic, had ivy-covered walls and ivory towers. In many ways they are still places for young people to *drop out of society*—places where students spend time reading, listening to lectures, and practicing skills away from the daily routines of life. Schools offer young people the time to drop out from the daily grind of working and making a living. Historically, schools were viewed as ways of keeping young people out of the workplace, even though vocational programs and career and technical schools were touted as preparation for that workplace.

Stemming the flow of dropouts and getting every young person on a path of productive learning will require that schools tackle the issue of student disengagement. Until schools deal with students' estrangement from their schools, they will continue to overlook talent, waste energy on compliance, and force students to fit into an increasingly archaic learning system.

In 1988, the William T. Grant Foundation issued two reports that addressed the needs of what was then identified as "the forgotten half": young people who did not go on to college after high school. Twenty years later, in *The Forgotten Half Revisited: American Youth and Young Families, 1988–2008*, Samuel Halperin (Bailey and Smith Morest 1998) reported that "there has been scant progress in a few areas and quite substantial regression elsewhere" (abstract).

We believe that our nation's high schools and colleges harbor another "forgotten half," a veritable fifth column of students dangerously disengaged from their schools and from productive learning. U.S. schools are not alone in experiencing this problem. A Canadian Education Association report on social, academic, and intellectual engagement (Willms, Friesen, and Milton 2009) found fewer than half of Canadian students were deeply engaged in their schools. Keeping these students in school through graduation and engaged in productive learning will require closer attention to students' expectations and the reasons they drop out of school.

Chapter

# 2

# HIGH HOPES

## STUDENTS' EXPECTATIONS

*Nobody succeeds beyond his or her wildest expectations unless he
or she begins with some wild expectations.*

—Ralph Charell

You would need to have been living under a rock during this last decade to miss hearing the phrase "high expectations." It was proclaimed about ten years ago by President George W. Bush in announcing the No Child Left Beyond initiative (The White House 2009), and it is earnestly echoed by policy makers and educational leaders to this day. We, however, remain perplexed as to how a narrow focus on reading and math scores—with a little science on the side—constitutes "high expectations."

In 1960, the theme song for JFK's presidential campaign was "High Hopes." Like JFK, young people have high hopes and expectations for themselves, and they also have high expectations of their schools and teachers. These expectations are often overlooked in the attention given to society's high expectations of students, teachers, and schools. Based on our work with young people and the reasons they disengage from school, we have identified ten expectations, phrased as questions from a student's perspective, that we believe are indispensible conditions schools must provide if they are to engage students in productive learning:

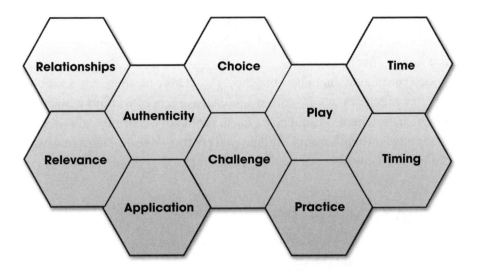

- **Relationships:** *Do my teachers and others who might serve as my teachers know about me and my interests and talents?*

- **Relevance:** *Do I find what the school is teaching to be relevant to my interests?*

- **Authenticity:** *Is the learning and work I do regarded as significant outside school by my communities of practice and by experts, family, and employers?*

- **Application:** *Do I have opportunities to apply what I am learning in real-world settings and contexts?*

- **Choice:** *Do I have real choices about what, when, and how I will learn and demonstrate my competence?*

- **Challenge:** *Do I feel appropriately challenged in my learning and work?*

- **Play:** *Do I have opportunities to explore—and to make mistakes and learn from them—without being branded a failure?*

- **Practice:** *Do I have opportunities to engage in deep and sustained practice of those skills I need to learn?*

- **Time:** *Do I have sufficient time to learn at my own pace?*

- **Timing:** *Can I pursue my learning out of the standard sequence?*

Even good traditional schools would find these expectations challenging, and most schools would see them as unreasonable, impractical, and simply unachievable.

Nevertheless, the failure of schools to deliver on these expectations explains much about why young people leave school without a diploma or remain in school without engaging in productive learning. As we take a closer look at each—from a student perspective—recall what school was like for you. How did your school measure up to these expectations?

# RELATIONSHIPS

### DO MY TEACHERS AND OTHERS WHO MIGHT SERVE AS MY TEACHERS KNOW ABOUT ME AND MY INTERESTS AND TALENTS?

Young people come to know who they are and who they want to become in large part through their relationships with others. They crave affiliation and aggressively seek it. They look for people, places, and circumstances that fulfill them. They join learning communities and communities of practice in and out of school. Because their teachers are significant persons in their lives, students crave a relationship with these mentors and coaches. Schools often fail to exploit the power of this drive. Indeed, at this critical juncture in a young person's development, schools typically step away from their students.

Most of us can remember one or two special teachers who did fulfill our "great expectations," but the culture, structure, and protocols of most schools make this kind of knowing and caring on the part of teachers challenging and burdensome. Abraham Maslow, famous for his hierarchy of needs, observed that often a fear of knowing is a fear of doing (Kaplan 1998). In-depth knowledge about students and their interests creates obligations teachers may find difficult to ignore. Even the most committed teachers might object to taking on so much responsibility. What preparation and competence do they have for dealing with homeless children or those on drugs or those with significant family issues? It might be better not to know, not to reach out.

When schools cannot respond to these expectations, young people seek other places and people who can give them what they need. When safe and positive out-of-school places and people are unavailable, many youth join gangs, use drugs, and perpetrate other mischief, much of it preventable.

In Big Picture Learning and similar schools—EdVisions Schools (www.edvisions.com), High School for the Recording Arts (www.hsra.org), and Maya Angelou Schools (www.seeforever.org), for example—students are encouraged, often required, to tell their teachers about themselves and their interests and aspirations. In a ninth-grade Big Picture Learning module titled Who Am I? students reflect on their interests, talents, and strengths and share their career aspirations as they relate to work, family, and community. From these reflections, teachers learn how issues of race, gender, and class impact students' interests and career aspirations. They learn how to help students enter and flourish in learning communities.

Young people are also attempting to answer *who am I?* on Facebook and other social networks. Adopting various avatars and personas, they reach outside and inside.

Some educators disagree with the importance we place on relationships. They believe it is better to focus on helping each student master the curriculum, do well on tests, and get good grades. They know students through their grades and test scores and shortcomings. Knowledge like that can be used to allocate scholarships and awards, but it yields little understanding about a student. How can a teacher *without* this understanding help students learn? Altering a school's culture and organization lets us achieve the right sorts of relationships.

# RELEVANCE

**DO I FIND WHAT THE SCHOOL IS TEACHING TO BE RELEVANT TO MY INTERESTS?**

How many times, as you sat in your classes, did you say, *I'll never use this in real life and in the work I want to do*? The eager-to-be engaged student asks, *Once you know about me, do you make an effort to use what you know to engage me in productive learning? To build on my strengths? To develop my talents? Do you help me see what you are teaching as helping me achieve my career and life aspirations?*

Relevance is a powerful way to engage reluctant learners. One of our Big Picture Learning students interned at a small local airport for four years. He was always making stuff—wooden bowls on lathes, pens, go-carts, and so on. Through an internship, he learned how to repair and maintain plane engines and fuselages, studied for his pilot's license, and became an integral part of the airport mechanic/engineer/maintenance team. He was hired to work summers, vacations, and beyond his internship hours. He is now in school to become a certified diesel mechanic.

Another student was interested in medicine and in becoming a physician. In junior year she took a biology class at the local university. In her senior year, she was selected to help the university biology faculty conduct original research on leishmaniasis, a parasitic disease soldiers have contracted in the Persian Gulf. She was part of the team attempting to find potential genetic markers associated with particular parasites and contributed to conference publications. She is now a scholarship student in the university's honors program. Neither of these students would probably have stayed the course in a traditional school. Addressing their interests turned them into productive learners.

Striving for relevance does not mean the school cannot teach anything unless the student finds it relevant. But it should at least force an attempt to make some connection to every student.

Young people's career interests evolve rapidly. They go from wanting to be a surgeon to a fireman to a dancer in a matter of months. They eventually decide on one, some as early as high school, others perhaps not until they have their first full-time job. Facilitating that discovery and decision is a school's responsibility.

Shannon, an Aboriginal young man in Victoria, Australia, said of his former school, "I had no teachers to help. I couldn't help myself because I couldn't get help." After he found a Big Picture Learning school that tailored instruction around his interest in design, there was no looking back.

"Now," reports his teacher, "he is designing. He does film and TV. He's in demand." Shannon has become a productive learner.

Relevance begins with the individual learner but need not end there. Learning flourishes when the learner engages the larger world and wants to learn more. Relevance acknowledges the deep connections between the student, his or her emerging interests in given areas, and the complex learning challenges that define those areas. Schools need to figure out ways for students to bring their interests into the school and then nurture these interests into the lifelong interests and careers they will pursue in the workplace, the family, and the community.

SCHOOLS NEED TO FIGURE OUT WAYS FOR STUDENTS TO BRING THEIR INTERESTS INTO THE SCHOOL AND THEN NURTURE THESE INTERESTS INTO THE LIFELONG INTERESTS AND CAREERS THEY WILL PURSUE IN THE WORKPLACE, THE FAMILY, AND THE COMMUNITY.

# AUTHENTICITY

**IS THE LEARNING AND WORK I DO REGARDED AS SIGNIFICANT OUTSIDE SCHOOL BY MY COMMUNITIES OF PRACTICE AND BY EXPERTS, FAMILY, AND EMPLOYERS?**

Recall your school experience. Did you feel at times that you were in a restaurant being fed the menu rather than what's *on* the menu? The settings, people, places, and contexts of school are at best fake-real, scripted like reality television. In school, most experiences are indirect, and students have no firsthand experience with real-world mysteries and problems. The curriculum's scope and sequence don't reflect the way knowledge and skills are used in the real world. We all remember the endless word problems and grammar exercises that seemed so unlike what real professionals do. These features of schooling contribute to its being seen as a form of disengagement from the real world.

Young people ask their schools to provide authentic learning experiences. They want assurances that these experiences will help prepare them for success in their future work and careers. We have collected many examples of this kind of authentic learning.

Seana wanted to understand the impact of recreation on children who live in public-housing developments (she lives in one) and use that understanding to make a difference. Her teachers helped her refurbish a neglected basketball court in her development. Seana learned important academic skills during this process and, equally important, developed her social skills by interacting with community agencies and businesses.

Justin has autism and is interested in education generally and autism specifically. During his sophomore year he did an internship with a charter school development agency. In his junior year, Justin worked with children with autism at an elementary school. As part of his senior thesis project, Justin organized an autism walk. These projects incorporated academic requirements. In Justin's words, "I have been at two elementary schools for half of my junior year and all of my current senior year. I am doing a Heritage Faire with fourth, fifth, and sixth graders. The purpose is for members of the school community to learn more about different cultures in an authentic way."

In a February 2005 article in *The Atlantic*, "Lost in the Meritocracy: How I Traded an Education for a Ticket to the Ruling Class," Walter Kirn describes the absence of authenticity in his education. He was a great test taker who went off to Princeton and realized what he didn't know and why:

> I've been fleeing upward since age five, learning just enough at every level to make it, barely, to the next one. I'm the system's pure product (para. 17). . . . I gave no thought to any goal higher or broader than my next report card. Learning was secondary; promotion was primary. No one had ever told me what the point was, except to keep on accumulating points, and this struck me as sufficient. What else was there? (para. 14)

This judgment might be echoed by many a valedictorian adept at taking tests and otherwise gaming the system.

Karen Arnold, an associate professor at Boston College, testifies to similar realities in her study of high school valedictorians, *Lives of Promise* (1995), and educational historian and Harvard University President James Bryant Conant (1940) long ago chastised schools for their *un*reality:

"Book learning" is placed too high in the scale of social ratings by some; too low by others who profess to scoff at "brains." That type of ability which can handle easily the old-fashioned subjects of the curriculum is often glorified by being equated with intelligence by educational snobs. . . . As a result, we have a great deal of make-believe in our schools and colleges—too many feeble attempts at tasks which are proper only for a restricted type of individual; too many failures to explore talents which fall outside orthodox academic bounds. (Section III)

# APPLICATION

### DO I HAVE OPPORTUNITIES TO APPLY WHAT I AM LEARNING IN REAL-WORLD SETTINGS AND CONTEXTS?

Application cements skill and understanding, and not just any application will do—it must be authentic. Application in real-world settings and contexts ensures that students are ready for lifelong learning and work. Application helps them "see" their learning and typically results in tangibles—products and performances that can be observed and evaluated by the students, their teachers, and others. Students want firsthand experiences in which to develop competency, and they want those experiences to mirror the way professionals in the real world think, perform, and learn. Students want to use what they learn—skills as well as understanding—to address real problems and challenges.

Consider the experience of two Big Picture Learning students. Julian always wanted to be able to write songs but didn't know how. He searched for a computer program that would help him, and when he couldn't find one, he began to create his own. Now a tenth grader, he is negotiating with Hasbro, the toy company, to develop and market his product. Allison wanted to become a police officer. She interned with a detective, in a patrol car, observing responses to real drug busts and accidents. She wanted to learn how inner-city teens' attitudes toward the police differed from those of teens in the suburbs. She conducted a statewide survey, with surprising results: suburban teens had a more negative attitude toward police than inner-city teens did. The key to developing good relations between police and teens was exposure. When police were a presence in schools and community centers, students' attitudes and relationships with police were positive. The City of Providence Police Department and our school in Providence used the results of this survey to guide relationships between police and students.

Schools must provide opportunities for students to take the learning developed in school and apply it outside school. They must also provide opportunities for students to bring learning they have accomplished outside school into school.

# Choice

### Do I have real choices about what, when, and how I will learn and demonstrate my competence?

Students want choices in what they learn and when and how they learn it. *Can I lead with my strengths? Can I focus on getting really good at something I value?* Often, young people look back on their high school experience and say, *I wish my school had offered a course in such-and-such.* Increasingly, however, more and more schools focus on a tight curriculum, with few opportunities for student choice. Students feel pushed away by the meager menu of options. Students with low test scores often have even fewer choices, because they must focus on raising those test scores.

Research on locus of control demonstrates how essential student voice and agency are in productive learning. Students need to make choices and accept responsibility for their choices. Placing unnecessary restrictions on young people inhibits their ability to do so. Failing to provide choices is particularly unfortunate when students have special talents that could be developed in school.

Schools fit all students to the same Procrustean bed, heedless of the "limbs" they may be chopping off to make each student fit the school's agenda: in the process they ignore important aspects of who students are. One of our Big Picture Learning students suffered head trauma in an auto accident as a young boy. As result, he couldn't focus well in school. By the time he reached high school, he hated school but loved ⌐ business cutting wood, and helped run heavy equipment on construc.. sites. He interned with a custom auto designer/builder for three years, helping to design and shape the bodies of and tune and build engines for cars worth hundreds of thousands of dollars. He ended up spending two days a week at his internship/business (seasonal) and three days at the school to document his projects and sharpen his math and literacy skills. He graduated and is now working. He has become accomplished in several skills and has the certificates to validate his skills and himself as a learner.

Common sense tells us that the uniqueness of each student requires a unique response to her or his learning needs. Providing different students with the same learning opportunities and learning environments is *not* giving them the same chance for success. Schools must have the courage to stand up for each student and create a unique program of study wrapped around his or her interests, one in which the student fully understands the responsibility of being part of the learning community. Abraham Lincoln's notion of equity—getting each person unstuck from rung after rung on the sticky ladder of upward mobility—is a fitting guide for such choices (Sandburg 2007).

> SCHOOLS MUST HAVE THE COURAGE TO STAND UP FOR EACH STUDENT AND CREATE A UNIQUE PROGRAM OF STUDY WRAPPED AROUND HIS OR HER INTERESTS.

# CHALLENGE

### DO I FEEL APPROPRIATELY CHALLENGED IN MY LEARNING AND WORK?

Young people seek out and embrace challenges outside school that they see as relevant and push themselves toward excellence. They expect to be pushed to the edge of their competence in school as well—and to be provided with the support necessary to learn at that edge.

Authentic challenges provide the scope and depth of real-world rigor. Great teachers deliberately promote rigorous learning and rigorously incorporate discipline and cross-discipline knowledge and skills into real-world contexts. Students want and need many opportunities to discover what excellence looks like in the real world.

Ruth's mother is Haitian, but Ruth, a student in a Big Picture learning school, had never been to Haiti to meet her family. After the 2010 earthquake, Ruth connected with a physician who ran a faith-based clinic in Haiti and supported a combination orphanage-school as well. Twice Ruth raised the money to buy her own ticket and went with Dr. Tom and his group of volunteer physicians to work in the clinic in Haiti. For her senior thesis, she produced a documentary about the clinic, the aftermath of the earthquake, and her finding and meeting her family for the first time. Ruth is now on full scholarship in a college premed program. Her ambition is to become a missionary doctor like Albert Schweitzer and her friend Dr. Tom.

# PLAY

### DO I HAVE OPPORTUNITIES TO EXPLORE—AND TO MAKE MISTAKES AND LEARN FROM THEM—WITHOUT BEING BRANDED A FAILURE?

Students like to play. They want opportunities to mess around and experiment in their learning and work. We are not talking about having fun, at least not exclusively, although a bit of that is great as well. We are talking about having the time to explore, experiment, and discover. Learning how to do that productively is difficult because the organizational structures and cultures of most schools are antithetical to messing around.

All innovators, from Edison to Einstein, tell us that mistakes made through play are powerful ways of learning. Mihaly Csikszentmihalyi (1996) writes that flow is achieved when work looks like play. Play has challenges, but the risks are low and the opportunities for recovery are many.

Play is at the heart of innovation and creativity, freeing the mind to invent. James Bernard Murphy (2011), professor of government at Dartmouth College, has written, "children are liberated from the grim economy of time. Children become so absorbed in fantasy play and projects that they lose all sense of time. For them, time is not scarce and thus cannot be wasted" (para. 9). However, some educators argue that regimentation and a focus on skills development are what the real world demands. It can't be all fun and games, as it was in kindergarten. As early as the first grade, these people say, students need to get prepared for the harsh realities and demands of the real world.

But the reality is that schools look less and less like the real world of learning and work. The most successful companies are striving to increase purposeful (and even not so purposeful) play into their organizations and cultures to spark creativity and invention. Stories abound about successful and admired companies that offer play, exploration, and interest-focused learning and work as a means of keeping and growing their employees and thereby growing their corporate bottom lines. Their efforts remind us of Nietzsche's observation, "The struggle of maturity is to recover the seriousness of the child at play" (Lehrer 2011).

Tinkering is a powerful form of play, and Mark Thompson (2011), a colleague from Australia, provides an excellent description of its connection to productive learning:

> Tinkering is a minor risk-taking activity without any great consequence. . . . It is not goal directed, nor are there defined outcomes. There are no key performance indicators for tinkering. . . . It is research without a known outcome. . . . [Tinkering] involves a flow state, which is a sort of an intense focus on a small, closed world. . . . An activity with these qualities runs counter to an awful lot of institutional trends of modern life. Tinkering and play are closely linked: a certain sense of wonder propels the curiosity at the heart of every compulsive tinkerer. Tinkering also allows for failure, an essential component of any process of evolution. *The pleasure in handling things is hardwired into us.* Tinkering gives tinkerers a powerful sense of the possibility of things, which surely must be a wellspring of creativity.

The best teachers use play to develop higher-order thinking (in which we include tinkering, or "thinkering"). Their learning opportunities are full of what ifs and why nots. They provide a bit of serendipity in their work with students and focus on exploration, thinking differently, and how-might-we problem solving.

# PRACTICE

### DO I HAVE OPPORTUNITIES TO ENGAGE IN DEEP AND SUSTAINED PRACTICE OF THOSE SKILLS I NEED TO LEARN?

---

PRACTICE IS A COMPANION TO PLAY.
. . . MESSING AROUND, TINKERING,
AND PLAY ALLOW YOUNG PEOPLE TO
TRY THINGS OUT WITH LOW RISK.

---

Practice is a companion to play; its focus is less on discovery and exploration and more on honing skills and performances. Practice entails deliberate attention to failing and learning from mistakes, often guided by images of quality and craftsmanship in performance and product. Sir Ken Robinson (2001) reminds us that the development of creativity requires a willingness to be wrong. Messing around, tinkering, and play allow young people to try things out with low risk. Our guess is that Robinson would have us treat play and practice as one, but we prefer to honor their subtle but distinctive features.

"The most powerful drive in the ascent of man is his pleasure in his own skill," observed Jacob Bronowski in *The Ascent of Man* (1976). "He loves to do what he does well, and having done it well, he loves to do it better" (para. 15). This is the essence of craftsmanship and excellence that Richard Sennett celebrates in *The Craftsman* (2008), noting that craftsmanship requires a form of practice that combines skill, commitment, and judgment.

Malcolm Gladwell (2008), citing research, reports that expertise requires approximately ten thousand hours of practice. And not just any form of practice will do. In *The Talent Code* (2009), Daniel Coyle describes high-quality practice as chockfull of small mistakes that get corrected immediately in a steady stream of do-assess-redo. This is the practice we often see in a school's arts wing and playing fields but seldom in its classrooms. Why is that? Could it be that no one sees the need for practice when the performance is neither relevant nor authentic? Or when trial and insight are viewed as unwanted and messy variation?

Students want expert practitioners to guide them in their practice. They want to learn how to practice well. They want the experience of going deep into a content area or the mastery of a specific skill. They want to make mistakes "early and often," as the experts advise, without being punished with poor test scores and grades. Schools need to regard mistakes made in practice as approximations of success and "smart failures," as many successful organizations describe them.

# TIME

### DO I HAVE SUFFICIENT TIME TO LEARN AT MY OWN PACE?

In *The Age of Unreason* (1990), Charles Handy provides an insightful example that illustrates the problem schools have with time. Imagine, he says, that you go to work in the morning and start working in your office or cubicle. After about an hour, a bell rings, you pack up your work and go to another office down the hall and begin work on a completely different project. Imagine that you repeated that sequence five or six times all day, every day. How much productive work, Handy asks, are you likely to accomplish? And we ask, how much productive learning would you expect to engender with such a system?

Students differ considerably in the time it takes them to learn something, yet a rigid schedule governs schools. Teachers are forced to move briskly through the curriculum, carrying every student along on the same schedule, leaving no time for interesting digressions or reflection.

John Thackera, author of *In the Bubble: Designing in a Complex World* (2005), observes that "multiple tempos—some fast, some slow—can coexist, but they have to be desirable, and they have to be designed" (48). We think both students and their teachers would value Thackera's concept of time, but the school's rigid schedule makes it impossible to attain. So what do students do when they know they don't have enough time? They sense immediately this is not the way things are done in the real world and proceed to fake it, learn and forget it, or worse, cheat. Great schools strive for depth of understanding rather than curriculum coverage, seek effectiveness before efficiency, and use time flexibly. They provide not just time for learning but time to grow and to understand how long it takes to do something well.

Here is another way of thinking about time. One of our Big Picture Learning students in Rhode Island had been hell on wheels for almost three years. She then had an opportunity to travel to South Africa to study apartheid. It transformed her. The trip was right for her. She was developmentally ready to grow. She came back, traveled to the Deep South on a civil rights historical tour, and spent her senior year serving on the governor's commission studying racial profiling by police departments in Rhode Island. She went on to college.

> OUR GREATEST TASK IS TO BUY STUDENTS SOME TIME TO GROW INTO THEMSELVES WITHOUT GIVING UP ON THEM.

Our greatest task is to buy students some time to grow into themselves without giving up on them. This is the reality that a lockstep schedule denies. Many young people who are struggling in school and leaning toward leaving would benefit from more creative uses of time for learning.

# TIMING

### CAN I PURSUE MY LEARNING OUT OF THE STANDARD SEQUENCE?

Students want to control timing as well as time. They want schools to see time and timing as variables to be exploited in accommodating their need for practice and play and their need for just-in-time rather than just-in-case learning. Yet schools act as if learning opportunities come only once. For example, schools believe students who do not learn algebra in high school are doomed to failure and will never have another opportunity.

The standard curriculum's scope and sequence provide a rigid grade-by-grade script for what is taught and when—another of those Procrustean beds that characterize schools. Yet, John Elder Robison (2011) reminds us, "the word 'delay' means what it says—late. Delayed does not mean never, no matter how much it may feel like that at age fifteen or even twenty-five" (23).

Sarason's Law, formulated by our mentor and muse, Seymour Sarason (2004), illustrates many powerful ideas, one of them focused on timing. The law postulates that teachers can teach reading or math only when the child wants to learn to read or do math. Sarason's reasoning was that once teachers focus on their students' interests, the students will be eager to understand more about what they are doing and will want to learn to read or do math. Imagine what teachers might do with their students to bring them to demand to learn how to read!

Uno Cygnaeus, father of the Finnish public school system (and the creator of *sloyd,* a system of hand-mind training still in use today) (Encyclopedia Britannica 2012), influenced Sarason, as did John Dewey and other education leaders around the world. In Finland, schools do not teach reading until the second grade. Instead, the early school years are devoted to play and making things (Anderson 2011, Hancock 2011).

# REASONABLE QUESTIONS ALL

There you have it: ten expectations that, consciously or not, students crave and that most schools largely ignore, arguing that these expectations are far too idealistic. Nevertheless, in the worlds of vocation and avocation, providers of out-of-school learning are listening carefully to students' expectations and improving their ability to deliver. Indeed, we think that social entrepreneurs will begin to treat these expectations as design requirements for developing alternative learning programs that address the user's experience. (Whether the schools we have can create alternatives to themselves based on these expectations is the subject of Chapters 9 and 10.)

> SOCIAL ENTREPRENEURS WILL BEGIN TO TREAT THESE EXPECTATIONS AS DESIGN REQUIREMENTS FOR DEVELOPING ALTERNATIVE LEARNING PROGRAMS THAT ADDRESS THE USER'S EXPERIENCE.

These expectations—essential conditions—for productive learning are much more easily addressed if schools take advantage of the world outside school, where young people find adults who are doing the work the young people wish to do and emulate these mentors in developing the necessary habits and practices.

Failing to address any one of the expectations could be a deal breaker for a young person already leaning toward leaving. Yet fulfilling even one or two of these expectations might be enough to keep some of those "leaners" engaged. Then, too, each student expectation works in tandem with the others. Addressing relationships, relevance, and authenticity, for example, allows teachers to challenge students to produce high-quality learning and work. Meeting these expectations allows teachers to expand students' interests to include the relevant aspects of all disciplines.

As you read the stories in this book by and about our students, you may be thinking that the schools these young people attend are very different from the schools you know. You may not have had learning opportunities similar to the ones described, many of them in out-of-school settings. You're right. The design of Big Picture Learning schools is unusual, and implementing this design is a challenge, since it requires so many fundamental changes in a school's organization, culture, programs, and curriculum. You may also find yourself thinking, "Yes, I agree that students' expectations are reasonable, but the schools we have cannot meet them." If so, you are ready to appreciate the fundamental changes educators need to make in the schools we have. And you are ready to take some steps toward fulfilling at least some of students' expectations.

Chapter

**3**

# LEANING TOWARD LEAVING

## HOW YOUNG PEOPLE DISENGAGE FROM THEIR SCHOOLS

*Just because you leave does not mean that your
education is necessarily interrupted.*

—RALPH CAPLAN

Roger Martin is dean of the University of Toronto's Rotman School of Management, Canada's mash-up of the MIT Sloan Management School and the Harvard Business School. The school has a distinguishing and distinguished emphasis on design thinking. Martin (2009b) is a world-renowned expert in the business of design and the design of business (the title of one of his recent books).

We have followed Martin's insightful work for several years because we share a mutual interest in using design thinking to produce innovative policies, programs, and practices that engender productive learning, whether it takes place in a classroom, a workplace, or the community. He told us this interesting story:

> I came from the top end of a dutiful family, so I survived grades 1–13
> (I was in Ontario when it had grade 13) because I was highly dutiful.
> I had only four courses in those 13 years that captured my

imagination—grade 12 and 13 history (thanks to Mr. Huschka) and grade 12 and 13 English (thanks to Mr. Exley).

But because of birth order dynamics, my youngest brother (fourth of five children) was not dutiful at all and was bored out of his proverbial gourd with secondary school. Thankfully my mother recognized this and let him stay home from high school whenever he wanted—writing notes to the vice-principal declaring: "Terry was not at school yesterday." In due course, she was called in to the VP's office to have it explained to her that the idea of needing a parent's note to justify one's absence from class actually meant a note with some justification, not just a note. Bless her, mom simply begged to disagree and asked to see the board of education rule, which just specified a note. (She was a former elementary school teacher.)

Fortunately for his two best friends, Joyce Gladwell (mother of Malcolm Gladwell) and Mrs. Headlam (mother of Bruce Headlam) followed suit, and the three irrepressible boys managed to get through high school going only as often as they could muster up the enthusiasm, but none of the three ever missed a class by Huschka or Exley. In fact, they sat at Mr. Exley's feet like three "grasshoppers" soaking up whatever they could possibly extract (check out the Nihilist Spasm Band if you want some background on Bill Exley). The three graduated from a regional high school in a town of 7K, and that didn't stop them from fame and fortune—Malcolm is, of course, Malcolm [Gladwell]; Terry [Martin] is the George F. Baker Professor of Russian Studies at Harvard University, and Bruce Headlam is a senior editor at the *New York Times*.

But had they not had (1) each other; (2) my ringleader mother; and (3) the incomparable Bill Exley, they could have all been dropouts. (Martin 2009a)

These three young men, aided and abetted by a wise mom, found ways of disengaging from most of what their school offered while deeply engaging in their selected interests.

We have come to view dropping out as a process of estrangement, a psychological and sometimes physical separation from school. While the lion's share of attention is typically given to potential and actual dropouts, schools need to look more closely at the nature of the disengagement that many more students experience, a situation that leads some students to break off the relationship entirely and drop out.

Like the estrangement that characterizes most failing and failed relationships, readily distinguishable stages and a seemingly infinite number of variations occur in the process of school disengagement. Some students recognize that the relationship with their school isn't working but decide to hunker down and stay the course. Others develop a "second life," including learning interests outside school and managing their in-school and out-of-school lives without ever bringing them together. Still others leave the relationship completely, pushed out by intolerable circumstances or pulled out by more compelling relationships and opportunities outside school.

Typically, the stages of disengagement unfold as a student moves from elementary to middle to high school, and we describe them that way here. But it need not always be so linear and gradual. While by law the act of dropping out must be delayed until age sixteen or later, it is possible to have students move through all three stages late in high school.

# "YOU'VE CHANGED"

Marriage counselors identify typical patterns in a relationship that is going bad. In the early stages, spouses discover that their common interests are fewer and less rewarding than they originally thought. Levels of trust, caring, and accommodation decline. Expectations of the relationship are not met and disappointment abounds: "You're not the person I married."

Many students go through a similar estrangement in their relationship with schools. The first experiences are typically positive, sometimes even joyful, with a focus on play, exploration, and building relationships. As early as the second or third grade, however, many schools drastically change the physical and psychological environment; rows of desks replace activity centers, and tightly structured and scripted instruction replaces exploration. The school's love for imaginative and playful students is replaced by a love for obedient and compliant ones. Schools change the learning opportunities and learning environments, thereby precipitating a break.

In the early stages of separation, many students discover that their interests and the school's do not align. They say, *This work that I am doing here is not me or mine. We don't want the same things.* At this point, the school repels these students, even though there may not be well-formed attractions for them outside school. Students' bodies and minds remain in school, but their spirits flag. They become disheartened because they aren't learning anything of interest. They do not own the learning they are asked to do, and intrinsic rewards are meager.

Despite this estrangement, many students still value the school's social networking and extracurricular activities and (like Roger Martin's "three irrepressible boys") the occasional "incomparable" teacher. Often, the most engaging student-teacher relationships are those that students have outside the regular school day with their coaches and club moderators.

However, schools fail to capitalize on their considerable advantages. In effect, they tell their students, *School is not about you, so put your dreams away. There is no time for dreaming or levity.* The school provides less time for play and less time for anything except the school's curriculum and its way of teaching: *It's my way or the highway.* Sadly, many students begin to consider that option. The estrangement at this early stage does not result in dropping out but often demonstrates itself in absenteeism, negative behavior, boredom, and poor grades. Students may feel they are not smart. They may feel lost and begin falling behind.

At this stage, students recognize that what matters to them does not matter to their school. Talented or not, their interests are ignored, and they see the school and its organization, curriculum, structures, and culture moving away from them. Few opportunities arise to bring their interests to school. Restrictions are built into every nook and cranny of the day. Teachers may ask *are you with me now?* but the question is usually rhetorical.

Many parents of young children observe with sadness their children's declining interest in what school has to offer. The romance of the earliest grades has suddenly faded. Researchers, particularly Mihayli Csikszentmihalyi (1997), have documented the decline of students' interest in school from kindergarten through high school.

Some students stay at this first stage of separation throughout their years in school. Theirs is often a passive disengagement, a marriage of convenience, if you will. They get passing grades and eventually graduate. Outside interests may form but are never a factor in the relationship. Typically, these students aren't detected by the school's early warning system targeting potential dropouts. Nevertheless, they seldom engage in the productive learning that should be at the heart of the relationship between young people and their schools.

## WHERE DID THE LOVE GO?

A relationship, particularly a failing one, seldom stays at rest. At some point, students look outside the school to form new affiliations. Often, this second stage of estrangement starts in the early middle grades, when most youngsters are struggling to figure out who they are as they go through significant physical and psychological changes. It can happen at any grade, however.

When students discover things other than school that they would rather be doing, their level of disengagement increases. This stage adds the pull of outside interests to the school's push away. The student's career interests and talents may not yet be fully formed, but aspirations to learn differently grow in intensity.

The pull of the outside can take many forms. Perhaps a student has an opportunity to travel, or the family has to move. Another student might be out of school for an extended period because of illness. For yet another, it might be sports, a hobby, or the opportunity to learn and work with adults and peers who share a passionate interest (an astronomy, computer, or art club; a dance studio; an automobile restoration garage). Such a student might be thinking, *I'm good at this and enjoy doing it and being with people who support me and share my interests.* It's normal for young people who have special talents (even if they're just emerging) to want to spend time developing them.

These natural tendencies threaten student-school relationships unless the school invites students to bring their interests to school with them—and then wraps a rigorous curriculum around these interests. But schools rarely do this, instead pushing students away from the relationship and squandering the opportunity to spark and develop those interests. With good intentions, schools stand their ground and stick to policies about seat time, course sequences, grade-level expectations, and other regulations. Just when students need more nurturing, schools "go academic," increasingly concerned about subject matter, grades, and especially testing. They introduce rigid schedules, bells, and classes taught by different teachers, none of whom has the time to know the students reasonably well. It appears schools are deliberately ignoring what is happening to the students they serve. As Auden (1938/n.d.), inspired by Bruegel, might have said of the schools, they "had somewhere to get to and sailed calmly on."

During this second stage the divergence of interests and focus increases significantly, and students may be leaning toward leaving. Schools fail to develop an emotional bond with their students. Trust weakens and both parties may begin cheating on each other, literally as well as figuratively. The rules of engagement are replaced by the rules of disengagement, and the relationship turns antagonistic. It's not hard to see a possible connection between this growing estrangement and the rise of student cheating—or even the cheating done by teachers and principals. We are not psychologists, but it is not much of a leap to assume a strong relationship between the pressure on educators to raise test scores and their own disengagement from their schools and perhaps from their students.

Many students linger in this stage, resigned to endure the estrangement, motivated perhaps by a few positives: the social environment, after-school activities, a great teacher, or a favorite subject. They realize, consciously or unconsciously, that they are not ready to leave school. Their performance might become spotty, and the schools' early warning systems may flag them as potential dropouts.

In *Landscapes of Betrayal, Landscapes of Joy*, Herb Childress (2000) documents his observations of young people who attend a North Carolina high school and notes the happiness the students experience outside school, where they can be themselves and pursue their interests, and the unhappiness they experience in school. These students maintain a kind of equilibrium between the pull of the outside and the push from the inside that develops because inside and outside learning cannot be blended.

Harry Lewis, the Harvard computer professor who taught both Mark Zuckerberg and, decades earlier, Bill Gates, had this to say about the Facebook CEO in the BBC documentary *Mark Zuckerberg: Inside Facebook*:

> The thing I would say about Zuckerberg is that he was very eager to learn and very skeptical about whether anything we were teaching him was actually the right thing for him to be learning. I think Bill Gates had exactly the same feeling. It was not disrespect for what was being taught, but maybe not exactly what he was interested in, [and] so on, so he was, you know, absorbing everything and not paying any attention to it at the same time. (British Broadcasting Company 2011)

This is student compliance at a high level—and a near perfect analysis of the situation! In this environment, the student is not paying sufficient attention to the professor, and neither the student nor the system sees it as a problem. The disengagement is built into the design and culture of the organization.

Our guess is that such disengagement is a basic feature of classrooms at every level of the K–12 enterprise. The student strikes a (rarely spoken) deal with the school: *I will do the minimum to keep the relationship intact, if you don't demand too much of me.* Students resign themselves to tolerating school. They sit in the classroom and somehow limp to a tainted graduation and a diploma that papers over their lack of readiness for successful postsecondary learning and work. They game the system only to find the system has gamed them.

Most of these students do not see themselves as disconnected, at least not from what matters. True, they are disconnected from school, but they are often connected to people, places, and objects outside school and are intent on expanding and diversifying these connections—connections that lead some students to make the final break. It is then that leaving-to-learn programs can interrupt the leaning-toward-leaving trajectory and leverage the pull of the outside to engage students and keep them from dropping out.

# "IT'S TIME TO SAY GOODBYE"

During this third stage, the relationship becomes intolerable for some students, and they begin to display unproductive learning and behavior. They misjudge how far to push the envelope and get into trouble by falling behind—or in some cases jumping ahead because they have already done the coursework. The situation becomes tense, testy, passive-aggressive, or just plain aggressive or passive. These students are otherwise engaged while going through the motions.

Contemplation turns to action when the tipping point is reached. The decision to physically separate morphs from subconscious to conscious. Sometimes this break is messy and fraught with anxiety. Here are Germaine's bitter words about such a push: "When I went to high school, they told me I couldn't take art class until I was a sophomore. The only thing they told me I could do that I liked was choose a language, but the only choice they gave me was French and I wanted Spanish, so I left." Another dropout reflected, "One thing was sure: by the time I left, they didn't want me, and I didn't want them. It was good riddance on both sides" (Robison 2011). With other students, the break is hardly noticeable—a quiet but nevertheless complete disengagement. Taking stock of their poor academic accomplishments and realizing that they have fallen too far behind ever to catch up, they throw in the towel and leave for different and, they hope, better prospects.

Discipline issues, family trouble, and substance abuse, among many other reasons, force some young people to leave school. Perhaps they need money for themselves or their families; perhaps a neighborhood gang pulls them away. Many of these events are too powerful for schools alone to address. As Richard Rothstein (2001) argues, schools as they are cannot overcome many of the life events and other circumstances that may overwhelm a young student.

In a conversation about leaving-to-learn programs with design consultant Ralph Caplan (2008), he told us, "Just because you leave does not mean that your education is necessarily interrupted. In fact, just the opposite could be occurring." Successful, sometimes famous, dropouts, like Bill Cosby, find a way to learn what they want and need to learn outside school. Michael Dell, Steve Jobs, Will Wright (creator of video games SimCity™ and Spore™), and Bill Gates left college and have received honorary college degrees not for the courses they took but for their learning and accomplishments outside school. In that new setting, their learning, as we have defined it, became truly generative and focused on craftsmanship, mastery, and artistry.

Others who reach this stage are less prepared and do not do well. In addition, the stigma of dropping out and leaving without a degree—in society's eyes, not finishing—creates a paradox even for dropouts who do go on to achieve success. Though proud of their accomplishments, they may feel that they are not quite as good or that they made the wrong decision. They bear this cross throughout their lives.

Reaching this last stage is definitely not a positive experience for the school or the students, but there is still hope for the relationship. Creating a leaving-to-learn program is a way to keep even students who are leaning toward leaving highly engaged in some form of productive learning.

For example, Susan "Suzy" Amis Cameron, former actress and model and the wife of director James Cameron, left school and moved to France to pursue a modeling career when she was very young (Harrington 2010). Later, in Los Angeles, her children's estrangement from their schools led her to create the Muse School of California, which focuses on igniting children's passion, creativity, global awareness, and concern for sustainability and community. The Muse School encourages its students to follow their interests, unleash their creativity, assume responsibility, and develop relationships in their community and supports them as they do so. The Muse School does not allow students to drop out of the real world; rather, it immerses them in it.

# RETHINKING THE RELATIONSHIP

This process of disengagement is not an anomaly. Systems theorists might see it as an emergent property of the traditional organization and culture of schools. Disengaging is a normal response to a relationship that is already pushing a student away. It is normal for young people to seek places and people that provide fulfilling relationships with rich language and communication, valued objects, and challenging but enjoyable activities. Remaining in unfulfilling relationships is unhealthy and can cause physical and emotional harm. Might the key to addressing the dropout problem, therefore, be *not* to address the dropout problem? It would certainly be easier.

The real problem, however, to tweak a phrase made popular by James Carville, President Clinton's former campaign advisor, is "*engagement*, stupid." The education system would have you believe that the only problem is dropouts, which can be solved by creating early warning systems that tag potential dropouts for special attention. But do not be deluded. This is an old magician's trick. The system has us watching the dropout issue while distracting our attention from the deeper and more pervasive problem of student disengagement.

Why?

Perhaps because focusing on the dropout problem does not require any fundamental change in the way schools operate. Life can go on as usual even as the school creates a special set of interventions for those students tagged by the schools' early warning system. The interventions typically turn out to be a larger dose of the same medicine more assiduously applied.

Such "cash-for-clunkers" programs, which treat the symptom rather than cure the disease, sometimes get the headline numbers moving in the "right" direction and allow bureaucrats to take credit for some immediate but tiny improvements. Like a fad diet that promises gain without pain, the mood boost we experience is short-lived, and it isn't long before another group of technocrats and social scientists comes along with another tweak to the system, often at great monetary expense. Student disengagement is the elephant we ignore at our peril. The situation recalls Nietzsche's (1882/2009) observation, "One hears only those questions for which one is able to find answers" (206).

The relationship between our nation's high schools and their students is going south at high speed. Plenty of evidence shows that a large percentage of the student body is partially or wholly disengaged. Many of the students passing the tests and earning the credits are not deeply engaged in productive learning. That is why so many high school graduates show up in college inadequately prepared to do well or show up in the workplace unprepared to contribute to the companies that hire them.

We are not advocates of dropping out of high school. The scores of famous and near-famous dropouts who achieved success do not convince us that dropping out is an attractive option. There may be rare instances in which dropping out of high school is the most positive step to take to jump-start productive learning. But such instances are hard to determine. Under what circumstances would you support a young person's decision to leave school permanently? What would you need to know about her or him? What do you think he or she would ask you to do to support his or her learning outside school? What alternatives would you provide?

Those who make it through to success by dropping out feel they are the exception, not the rule. They don't recommend dropping out, because it takes a special person with special talent. They are like Richie, who told his son he didn't have talent and should stay in school.

Pushing students to disengagement is not primarily a function of poor teaching. Rather, disengagement is built into the design of schools and schooling. This is school's blind spot. School's relationship with students is based unnecessarily on a sorting and weeding out process that may be appropriate for a sports team but is toxic for identifying and developing talent in young people. Hundreds of alternative schools around the country are attempting to change that toxic culture, but they

HUNDREDS OF ALTERNATIVE SCHOOLS AROUND THE COUNTRY ARE ATTEMPTING TO CHANGE THAT TOXIC CULTURE, BUT THEY ARE BANDAGES ON A SYSTEM THAT REQUIRES FUNDAMENTAL REDESIGN, SAFETY VALVES THAT INADVERTENTLY REDUCE THE PRESSURE FOR MORE FUNDAMENTAL AND WIDESPREAD REFORM.

are bandages on a system that requires fundamental redesign, safety valves that inadvertently reduce the pressure for more fundamental and widespread reform. Many of these schools rely on students coming back a bit older and more ready to put up with getting through to graduation, essentially settling in at stage two as we have described it. Rather than fundamentally redesigning what exists, the education system is kicking the can down the road.

Disengagement is not a phenomenon confined to young people in schools. Sociologists and other observers have noted the decline in engagement throughout our society. Adults, we learn, are less connected to their institutions and to one another. Estrangement is on the rise in the workplace, as ever larger numbers of workers report that their jobs are unfulfilling. And researchers have observed estrangement in society as well. In *Bowling Alone: America's Declining Social Capital* (1995), Robert Putnam documents the growing insularity in society that is diminishing several forms of social capital. Schools, therefore, may need to double down their efforts to develop healthy relationships with their students to meet their expectations and focus on productive learning.

Opportunities to learn outside school are growing in quantity and quality. Does that mean that many students who currently remain passively disengaged will choose those alternatives? Or will these alternatives allow them to make their school relationship stronger? Will the rules of engagement change?

# Engaging Students in Productive Learning

It makes little difference whether students learn in or out of school if that learning does not prepare them for success as lifetime learners in all their "careers" within the workplace, the family, and the community. The next three chapters address three perennial questions related to productive learning that not just educators but all members of society are attempting to answer:

1. **What constitutes success?**
2. **What is important to learn to achieve success?**
3. **How should schools help students learn productively?**

Our answers to these questions, which are neither definitive nor unchanging, guide our efforts to engage all students in productive learning.

We address the first question by describing the multidimensionality of success in the context of a young woman's first job interview.

In addressing the second question, we challenge the current, narrow definition of "high expectations" for students' learning and argue for much broader and deeper expectations, particularly with respect to the arts, creativity, and invention. We describe an alternative way of looking at standards and argue for more attention to the quality of learning—craftsmanship, mastery, and artistry.

In addressing the third question, we propose a framework for designing learning opportunities that address students' expectations and result in productive learning for all students. We draw on the ways that all sorts of successful people learn and work outside the formal school system. Looking outside schools helps us get beyond what is taken for granted about learners, learning, and schools.

Chapter

4

# WHAT CONSTITUTES SUCCESS?

*To be what we are, and to become what we are capable of becoming, is the only end in life.*

—ROBERT LOUIS STEVENSON

Our definition of productive learning is based on Seymour Sarason's (2004) notion that such learning must be generative—engendering a desire to learn more, more deeply. Productive learning also requires rigorous student work that focuses on competence (i.e., performances that demonstrate knowledge, skills, and dispositions) and leads the learner to pursue craftsmanship, mastery, and artistry.

With this definition of learning as our guide, we now share our sense of what constitutes success for K–12 students. Most would define it as good grades, great test scores, a high school diploma, and a pathway to postsecondary learning. While we do not argue with those indicators, our experience tells us they are inadequate. We prefer additional indicators from a wider perspective: obtaining enjoyable and productive work with good prospects for growth, raising a family, contributing to the community, and figuring out how to navigate life's ups and downs. Indeed, navigating is an appropriate metaphor, since success is better thought of as a journey than a destination. Like happiness, success is an ever emerging state that differs for each individual.

Here's a composite image of successful learning based on a number of graduates of Big Picture Learning schools (Mojkowski and Washor 2011).

Rachel is on her first serious job interview at a small local design firm specializing in creating new product ideas for the home. The lead interviewer says, "Although it does not appear on paper that you are qualified for the position, something about your résumé caught our attention. We have a few questions for you, but please start by telling us about yourself and your work."

Rachel jumps in. "Your firm specializes in designing products for homes. For the last three years I have been doing just that as part of my formal and informal learning. I have researched your company, and believe I understand your process, your products, and your customers. I'm eager to show you some of my designs and describe the process I use.

"But first I want to tell you a little bit about myself. You know I have a two-year technical degree in design. I know you think such a degree is inadequate preparation for the work you do. Nevertheless, I am confident that I am prepared to contribute to your company's success, perhaps not right away but definitely in the near future."

Rachel distributes a list of competencies she has used to guide her learning activities over the previous three years and summarizes her scores on basic literacy and numeracy. "You see my math scores aren't great. I struggled with algebra but let it slide when I realized how little I needed it in the work I wish to do. I can always learn it if I need to."

She then focuses on the competencies she knows are valuable to the design firm. "I'm particularly strong in design thinking, communicating through graphics and physical objects, working flexibly and adapting to change, and using technology to find and disseminate information. I have provided my performance scores in these areas. My portfolio shows how I have used those skills to create actual products. I also have video references on my iPad from two mentors in the industry you might know. And I've earned two certificates, developed by your industry, that validate my competence.

"I've also done some design work in the community. I led a small team that redesigned a community center for homeless people and contributed to the interior design of the new senior center."

Is Rachel a successful graduate? We think most high schools and community colleges would be proud to claim her as a former student. Would you predict that Rachel will do well in her career? We think so. But what if you were Rachel's algebra teacher? Your definition of Rachel's success might focus primarily on her learning in your class. Would you agree with her assessment of algebra's importance? It's so easy to see a student's success from only one perspective.

It's harder to predict Rachel's longer-term success as a family and community member, but most people would be optimistic here as well. Our point is that we need to be willing to consider a much broader definition of success than the one that currently guides schools in their design of learning opportunities for their students.

It is not just schools that need a more comprehensive understanding of success and how to achieve it. Our country is often of two minds about success. While most Americans celebrate the outliers who define success differently and take an unconventional path to achieve it, they (and this includes parents and education policy makers) take a very conservative and narrow view of what constitutes success with respect to schools and schooling. Parents, for example, are convinced that a four-year degree from as prestigious a college as their budgets will allow is the ideal pathway to success.

Our country and our schools need to treasure diversity, not just in ethnicity and race but also in how we look at the world and its problems and how we devise solutions to those problems. We are reminded of the poem "Pied Beauty," by Gerard Manley Hopkins (1877), in which he celebrates "dappled things. . . . All things counter, original, spare, strange." Hopkins encourages us to nurture the outliers.

Scott Page, in *The Difference: How the Power of Diversity Creates Better Groups, Firms, Schools, and Societies* (2007), makes both an ethical and a pragmatic case for embracing diversity. He states that organizations that create deliberately "dappled" work groups—populated by individuals who see and engage the world differently—reap the benefits of diversity. That is one reason, as Richard Florida (2005) and Edward Glaeser (2011) have found from their research, some cities are so rich economically and culturally—they support many forms of diversity and flourish as result.

OUR SCHOOLS AND OUR COUNTRY ARE WASTING TALENT BECAUSE OF OUR FAILURE TO EMBRACE THE "PIED BEAUTY" THAT DISTINGUISHES MANY OF OUR YOUNG PEOPLE.

It seems, therefore, actually dangerous or at least detrimental to our individual and collective well-being to stand so firmly on one definition of success. Our schools and our country are wasting talent because of our failure to embrace the "pied beauty" that distinguishes many of our young people.

Sir Ken Robinson (Ted.com 2006) tells the story of Gillian Lynne, whose inability at age eight to sit still and pay attention in class landed her in a psychologist's office only to discover that her "flightiness" was caused by her love of movement and dance. A supportive mom and an observant doctor saved Lynne and directed her to schools that nurtured and rewarded her "dappledness." She went on to attend the Royal Ballet School in Britain and became a world-renowned ballerina, dancer, and actor who choreographed the dances in *Cats* and *Phantom of the Opera*.

Embracing a broad definition of success and how to achieve it is a key requirement for creating more successful schools. And, as we argue going forward, using the learning opportunities and learning environments that the world outside schools provides in abundance will allow schools to nurture all of that pied beauty.

Chapter

# 5

# WHAT IS IMPORTANT TO LEARN TO ACHIEVE SUCCESS?

*It don't mean a thing if it ain't got that swing.*

—DUKE ELLINGTON AND IRVING MILLS

In addressing what needs to be learned to achieve the many and varied dimensions of success, we make several assertions:

- Schools address a dangerously narrow number of learning standards.

- Schools give little or no attention to creativity and invention.

- Schools' insistence that all students address all learning standards and address them in the same way is counterproductive and wasteful.

- Schools' focus on low levels of competence impedes the quest for mastery, craftsmanship, and artistry.

## AN UNCOMMON CORE

The Common Core State Standards Initiative has created a large compendium of "core competencies" that must be addressed to obtain a high school diploma. These standards, which have been adopted by nearly all the states, specify what every student must learn and, generally, when he or she must learn it to be ready to perform the coursework required in the first two years of college.[1]

In her interview, Rachel refers to competencies that don't usually appear on schools' lists. Most employers of a generation ago would not have valued some of the competencies she describes: design thinking, creative problem solving, and technological literacy. But the changes occurring in nearly every aspect of our society, particularly the workplace, require these and similar competencies. To be successful in the emerging society and economy, young people will need skills that previous generations did not. They will need to solve problems that do not have clear answers and that computers address poorly, if at all.[2]

Most students now entering high school will work in jobs that do not yet exist, in industries still in their infancy or not yet created. Our society and economy, therefore, need graduates who, when confronting a new challenge, can define its relevant dimensions, discover key information, identify the major questions and issues, understand and analyze the key opinions, make connections, and devise and apply solutions to the problem.

We are strong advocates for the competencies required in and across the disciplines. How does a lawyer, lab technician, farmer, artist, carpenter, or architect think, learn, and perform? How does anyone pursuing a career acquire and use new knowledge and skills? What dispositions are essential to making one's way in a career or in society? In our Big Picture Learning schools, we have found that developing social capital is a particularly important competency. How do young people join, learn from, and contribute to learning organizations, communities of practice, and the panoply of social networks that provide opportunities for lifelong learning, civic engagement, and work?

---

1. The Common Core State Standards Initiative is led by the National Governors Association Center for Best Practices and the Council of Chief State School Officers. See their website for more information: www.corestandards.org/.

2. We should not, however, get complacent. In *Race Against the Machine* (Digital Frontier Press 2012), Eric Brynjolfsson and Andrew McAfee report that the number of skills where humans outshine computers is diminishing rapidly.

The Common Core is singularly narrow and ignores a large body of knowledge and skills—creativity and invention, design thinking, entrepreneurship, integrating knowledge across multiple disciplines, and going deeply into an academic discipline toward mastery—that are absolutely essential for success.

While educational leaders vociferously advocate for "higher expectations," they give most of their attention to what they can measure easily (if not well)—mostly literacy and numeracy. All students being able to read and compute is *not* a higher standard when the world we are coming to— *the world we are already living in*—requires an uncommon core—essentials for success such as those listed in the previous paragraph. While schools universally extol the virtues of what are called twenty-first-century competencies, few schools systematically teach and assess them.

Sir Ernest Rutherford, the physicist credited with splitting the atom, once arrogantly quipped, "All science is either physics or stamp collecting" (Birks 1962, 108). Educators have decided that it's all about literacy, math, and science, and everything else is "stamp collecting." How very wrong schools are for neglecting so many other facets of students' intellects and ignoring the reality that all of us are also artists, fabricators, and fixers. (Rutherford was also wrong. If he had lived long enough, he would have witnessed the rise to prominence of the biological sciences while physicists were busy pushing superstrings.)

# NO HEAD FOR CREATIVITY

One important set of learning standards ignored by the Common Core is that relating to creativity and invention. The evolution of Mr. Potato Head is a fitting metaphor for what has happened and is happening to the development of creativity and invention in our schools.

Mr. Potato Head began life as the creation of Brooklyn native George Lerner, who as a young boy used to take vegetables from the family garden and make objects out of them for his siblings. Lerner's garden provided every imaginable body part. Spinach, carrots, peppers, broccoli, were transformed into hair, eyes, ears, noses. His Mr. Potato Head kits, sold to

Hassenfeld Brothers (now Hasbro) in 1952, were an outgrowth of these playful childhood activities. The first kits provided a variety of thirty plastic pieces—with the option to order fifty more—to stick into your real potato (or any fruit or vegetable) or the included Styrofoam head.

The inevitable devolution, dumbing down, from real to fake, prompted by concerns such as rotting potatoes, took place in due course. Mr. Potato Head's body became a hard plastic shell—no more need for the real-deal potato—and the nature of the challenge changed. In the 1970s, the predrilled holes became flat slots to signal where the parts must go and in what direction. To the dismay of budding Picassos, no longer could you put an arm where the eye should go (wasn't that half the fun?). Mr. Potato Heads could no longer, as the commercial stated, "look different every time you make them" (Mrpotatohead.net n.d., Walsh 2005).

The original Mr. Potato Head allowed children to use their hands, minds, and hearts to fashion and refashion an object they could animate—to build an open-ended narrative from their imagination. Today's Mr. Potato Head kit is more useful for assembling and collecting than for imagining and experimenting.

We said there's a metaphor. Our global competitiveness will not be ensured solely through higher literacy and numeracy, perhaps not even by producing more engineers. It will be ensured by a marked increase in our ability to create and invent. Only through creativity, invention, and innovation will we be able to, as renowned observer of organizations Peter Drucker (1995) advised, leapfrog our global competitors, and, we might add, revitalize our communities.

ONLY THROUGH CREATIVITY, INVENTION, AND INNOVATION WILL WE . . . LEAPFROG OUR GLOBAL COMPETITORS . . .

And so we look to the schools to prepare their graduates to bring important innovation competencies—creative problem solving, invention—to communities and workplaces and to address as well the arts, including music and dance. These competencies, however, are not part of the national focus on the Common Core State Standards. The school curriculum has gone the way of Mr. Potato Head. Educators have distilled out of it practically any attention to creativity and innovation. No messing around or tinkering is tolerated.

Educators blame inadequate resources for this lack of attention, but the explanation is much deeper. Schools have a constricted view of the role of the arts in all learning and how the arts should be taught. We are reminded of Elliot Eisner's (1985) and Howard Gardner's (1999) insight that other forms of knowing are as, if not more, valuable to individuals and to society. Sir Ken Robinson (2001) argues that the current cognitive-abstract curriculum is designed to produce college professors. The arts, crafts, and technical competencies are largely ignored and in some cases disparaged. Yet, these very competencies contribute to success, as they did for Rachel and for hundreds of other students in our schools.

You would be correct if you inferred that Rachel attended an uncommon school. Few schools would allow, much less aggressively support, the learning Rachel did. But such alternative models do exist in our and other countries. Some career-focused high schools in the United States provide such programs. In Big Picture Learning schools, for example, students spend two days a week in all kinds of workplaces working on projects focused on their interests. Finland's schools place the performing and the practical arts at the core of the curriculum and address important learning standards in a holistic instructional process. Their highly integrated curriculum addresses what U.S. schools consider separate academic and vocational tracks as part of one system, with many opportunities for students to learn within their interests. Finland's schools provide lots of opportunities for tinkering and making (Anderson 2011, Hancock 2011).

## ALL AND NOTHING

Is a basic core of competencies essential for every student? Must all students be competent in that entire core before you would consider them a success? Before you would consider them ready for postsecondary learning and a career? Rachel dismisses her poor algebra scores as not important in relation to her competence for and commitment to the work she wishes to do. Do you agree with her? Do you think the interviewing team cared?

We believe Rachel's interview team would say: *Forget about those math scores. Forget about algebra. We need your excellent design-thinking skills. We need your project management skills. We need your collaboration skills. Moreover, if you need to learn some algebra at some point in your career, there are numerous ways in which you can get what you need when you need it, in conjunction with the work you will be doing to make it meaningful and applicable.* Rachel's time is much too valuable for just-in-case learning when just-in-time learning resources are readily available. Education is not a one-chance, last-chance system. There is a lifetime of opportunities for learning—even for learning algebra!

Schools' insistence that success requires algebra at a specific grade constitutes a mindless disregard for the individual and her career aspirations. The algebra requirement displaced time that Rachel might have had for other more important learning. In an April 2010 *Education Week* article, Robert Lerman and Arnold Packer (2010) (the former an institute fellow at the Urban Institute and a professor of economics at American University in Washington, the latter an Assistant U.S. Secretary of Labor from 1977 to 1980 and the Executive Director of the Secretary of Labor's Commission on Achieving Necessary Skills, known as SCANS) state:

> Consider Algebra 2, the study of logarithms, polynomial functions, and quadratic equations. Although many states want to make the course a requirement for graduating from high school, there appears to be no need to do so. Northeastern University sociologist Michael Handel has found that only 9 percent of people in the workforce ever use this knowledge, and that fewer than 20 percent of managerial, professional, or technical workers report using any Algebra 2 material.

The reality is that few students will do well on all of the competencies. Tradeoffs will be made. Each student will, as Rachel did, discover what competencies are important for success in her further learning and career and add them to her lifelong learning plan, updating it regularly to reflect new demands and aspirations. This is important work for schools.

With respect to science, technology, engineering, and math (STEM), policy makers are particularly interested in increasing the number of high school graduates who are ready to move into science, technology, and engineering careers, reasoning that such a workforce will provide a significant and enduring stimulus for our country's anemic economy. Based on this reasoning, they direct extraordinary resources to schools that are willing to increase the number and quality of STEM programs and graduates.

We have no quarrel with improving math and science programs. We are wary, however, of policy makers and educators who, concerned about our country's competitiveness, seek to increase the number of scientists and engineers by requiring *every* student to follow a pathway of more, and more rigorous (by their definition), math and science courses while expecting that many students will disengage and perhaps even drop out of school.

Perhaps their reasoning is that requiring all students to enter the STEM pipeline as early as middle school will increase the number of high school graduates who drip out the other end ready to work in these areas. It's like forcing every child to play on middle and high school basketball teams to increase the number of NBA stars. What, however, of the student who wishes to pursue a different career path, say in the arts, law, or social service?

# HANDMADE STANDARDS

In addition to requiring that all students address all the standards, schools typically insist that they be addressed in the same way. Here's a true story—first told in a commentary we wrote in *Education Week* in 2005—that illustrates a way of thinking about standards and variation.

A young, talented, and recognized artist and potter, Chicky moved from London to New York City's SoHo neighborhood and opened a pottery store to display and sell her creations. One day, an agitated customer entered the store to return a set of dishes she had purchased a few days before. The customer demanded her money back because all the plates and cups weren't exactly the same. Chicky couldn't believe what she was hearing. "Look," she said, "that's the point. Handmade pottery pieces aren't exactly the same because they are handmade. If you wanted all the pieces to be the same, you should have gone to another store and bought manufactured china." Realizing that there was no use discussing the matter any further, Chicky returned the woman's money and took back the set of dishes.

This story can be applied to the standards debate in education. Some educators really want all the plates to be the same; others feel that standards are best reached by having them different, that is, handmade. Both groups see standards as the best way for ensuring that all students are guaranteed the opportunity to acquire knowledge, skills, and dispositions that the world really values.

We prefer to think about standards as Chicky does. Variation, not standardization, produces real-world learning, provides meaningful benefits to all learners—and to society. As the old Duke Ellington standard implies, you take a standard and you swing it. You give a standard life by giving it your style, your signature, your maker's mark. Rachel used her portfolio to display her special capabilities and particular perspectives on the learning and work she had already accomplished and proposed to do.

The prevailing focus in education on having all students meet the same standards in the same way and demonstrate their competence in the same way is giving standards a bad name. Instead, schools need a much more dynamic view of what is to be learned. They need to accept that there is no one canon with respect to content; there are many and diverse canons. There is far too much knowledge to be encompassed in one, unchanging body of need-to-know knowledge. Canons need to be created around careers and evolve to accommodate new knowledge and skills. Allowing variation is a key requirement for engaging students in productive learning.

# APPROACHING STANDARDS

Schools need to view standards as they are used in the real world—as benchmarks of quality to which learners aspire. Such standards in all life roles emerge from a deep engagement with the world to which those standards relate. Standards established by a panel of experts often have little or no reality for students, teachers, or the public unless those standards are connected to the real world in which performance against the standard is relevant.

What constitutes high quality in a student's learning and work? Certainly it is more than what is captured in a test score or a letter grade. Success requires attention to the quality of the learning as demonstrated through performances and products. Excellence is not static; it is dynamic. It's an aspiration—a quest much more than an endpoint—and typically missing from the learning process and, consequently, from much student work. Excellence has several important dimensions, among them, craftsmanship, mastery, and artistry (Washor and Mojkowski 2006–2007).

Many schools have embraced rigor as their quest, but it is not clear what increased rigor they are seeking. Most often schools seek increased rigor through a curriculum with more than the average requirements: four years of math and science rather than three, ten novels not five, more difficult problems in traditional tests and related assessments, and so forth.

Such expectations fall far short of the rigor students need to demonstrate. Curriculum developers and teachers—even students—often construe rigor narrowly, failing to encompass the scope and depth of authentic academic or career-focused work. These misunderstandings unduly constrict strategies for promoting teaching and learning in schools and underestimate how discipline and cross-discipline knowledge and skills can be applied in real-world contexts.

Our definition of rigor focuses on students' work. What student behavior signals that they are doing rigorous work, that they are pursuing excellence in the processes of thinking, performing, and learning?

Both academic and career-focused rigor involve deep immersion, over time, in sophisticated texts, tools, objects, and language in real-world settings or great labs, often working with a number of mentors—expert practitioners as well as expert theorists. In such settings, students—like academicians, artists, craftsmen, and clinicians who are rigorous about their work—encounter problems that are complex and for which tools and processes for solving them are usually not readily apparent or available. Their work is open to peer and public scrutiny.

Rigorous learning and rigorous work cause students to take some type of action, to develop their own questions, to notice, observe, and reflect. They learn how hard it is to do something well, that it's not just about delivering answers but about framing questions for oneself and then devising methods to answer them. The questions are important because students don't know the answers and can claim both the questions and the answers as their own. Through authentic projects students develop their self-awareness and own their ideas, actions, and products. They scrutinize and challenge original assumptions. They see their learning and work as never complete. Their experience is spontaneous, reflective, and intimate, simultaneously the quest of the artist and the scientist with their different ways of knowing and engaging the world and their work.

> THROUGH AUTHENTIC PROJECTS STUDENTS DEVELOP THEIR SELF-AWARENESS AND OWN THEIR IDEAS, ACTIONS, AND PRODUCTS. THEY SCRUTINIZE AND CHALLENGE ORIGINAL ASSUMPTIONS.

Rigor focused on competence may not be enough, however; going forward, the most challenging work will require craftsmanship, mastery, and artistry. Social scientist Richard Sennett (2008) discusses how craftsmanship manifests itself in performances and products. Craftsmanship, he explains, brings together skill, commitment, and judgment in a unique way. It can exist in all manner of work, in processes as well as products—in a letter to the editor, a simulation, a dance, or a lab report. Craftsmanship involves the body as well as the mind, the hand as well as the heart, resulting in what Ron Berger (2003) calls beautiful work, "building craftsmanship in work and thought" (65).

Craftsmanship takes time—long hours alone and with mentors and coaches. Although craftsmen address very high standards, each individual craftsman has his or her style and signature in interpreting the standard. Such a signature may inhere in a process, a product, or a performance and occurs in all fields of endeavor. A craftsman's way of performing and producing has variations but is also highly consistent with other practitioners of the same craft. This style resonates with other people and rewards both the craftsman and his or her customers or audience.

The journey to mastery is demanding and much different from the "mastery learning" typically taking place in schools. In the world outside schools, rigorous work that results in mastery is at the far end of competence and is achieved after years, even decades, of practice and performance. Malcolm Gladwell (2008) reminds us that ten thousand hours are required to approach mastery, but the number is less significant than the understanding that mastery requires a commitment to a life's work and typically requires practice—alone and with others—that is carefully coached and critiqued, typically by other masters.

Hilary Austen, in *Artistry Unleashed: A Guide to Pursuing Great Performance in Work and Life* (2010), speaks insightfully of mastery and artistry as the ultimate goals of rigorous learning. She helps us understand "how the hopeful and bumbling efforts of a beginner can transform into the flowing precision of advanced performance" (15). Austen maintains that when students are challenged to go beyond competence, they can move to "that state we call artistry, that state where the tentative plucking of notes becomes the compelling music that rouses our strongest emotions, or where the routine chopping of onions turns mere groceries into the aromas and flavors that make us drool" (17).

Kyna Leski (2012), dean of architecture at the Rhode Island School of Design, states that creativity is not in knowledge itself but in exploiting the multiple ways of knowing. Discovery and invention are not about arriving somewhere expected but about deliberately moving outside what is known. Artistry is about aesthetics embedded in performances and products that amaze with their elegance and simplicity and the pleasure they give.

Artistry, mastery, and craftsmanship require time in which to go deep, to understand how hard it is to do something well. Students need to employ such skills and dispositions in making their way in the world.

Peter Senge's (1990) description of personal mastery offers images of the young people we wish to graduate from our schools:

> Personal mastery is the discipline of continually clarifying and deepening our personal vision, of focusing our energies, of developing patience, and of seeing reality objectively (7). . . . [It] goes beyond competence and skills, though it is grounded in competence and skills. It goes beyond spiritual unfolding, although it requires spiritual growth (131). . . . [It] can also mean a special level of proficiency (7). . . . People with a high level of personal mastery share several basic characteristics. They have a special sense of purpose that lies behind their vision and goals. For such a person, a vision is a calling rather than simply a good idea (132).
>
> People with a high level of personal mastery live in a continual learning mode. They never "arrive." Sometimes, language, such as the term "personal mastery," creates a misleading sense of definiteness, of black and white. But personal mastery is not something you possess. It is a process. It is a lifelong discipline. People with a high level of personal mastery are acutely aware of their ignorance, their incompetence, their growth areas. And they are deeply self-confident. Paradoxical? Only for those who do not see that "the journey is the reward" (142).

HELPING EVERY STUDENT ALONG THE LIFELONG PATH TO PERSONAL MASTERY MUST BE THE GOAL . . . AND MUST CONSTITUTE THE "HIGH EXPECTATIONS" SCHOOLS HAVE FOR THEIR STUDENTS.

Helping every student along the lifelong path to personal mastery must be the goal of every school if we are to serve well the young people who need so much more than competence to achieve success. This quest must constitute the "high expectations" schools have for their students.

The story of a recent graduate of one of our schools illustrates the journey that Senge describes. At his previous high school, Carl struggled with many challenges, and his education stalled. Advised that his best option was the Army or Job Corps, Carl withdrew from the school and enrolled at a Big Picture Learning school. His advisor changed his life. He told Carl that he would be able to design his own education, choose how *he* wanted to learn. Carl had interests in medicine and politics, so he did an internship at the University of Colorado's Blood Cancer Research Laboratory, where they were doing research to prevent the growth of malignant cells. When he graduated, Carl was awarded a scholarship to any school in the country. He recently graduated from college with a social science major and a minor in political science, also having been president of his nursing class. After working in public health in the developing world he hopes to come back to the United States and start a health care organization that supports, educates, and treats patients with HIV. As he would tell you, there is a measure of sociology and political science behind the disease.

Carl is a benchmark for the students we wish to—need to—graduate from our schools—and unlike Rachel, he is not a composite. He likely would have remained a dropout, but he found a school and a program that helped him learn within his interests. Within that learning space, his advisor was able to challenge him to broaden his focus and reach for excellence.

To help all students succeed, schools need to address a much broader set of competencies stretching far beyond the current myopic focus, embracing the whole person—academic, thinker, inventor, fabricator, performer, entrepreneur, citizen—and moving beyond competence to craftsmanship, mastery, and artistry. Schools must address competencies relating to creativity and invention and allow (and preferably, aggressively support) variation in what standards are addressed and how. Challenging all students with such breadth and depth will require that we first engage them more deeply in such learning. And engaging them will require paying attention to their expectations.

Chapter

# 6

# HOW SHOULD SCHOOLS HELP STUDENTS LEARN PRODUCTIVELY?

---

*Many educators have hobbies and passions and quite often fail to look at their own behavior in those fields. Ask yourself how and why you enjoy learning more about something, whether it is cooking, politics, or stamp collecting. Then ask yourself if it is possible to bring some of that same behavior into the environment you are making for others to learn.*

—NICHOLAS NEGROPONTE

Our approach to helping students engage in productive learning and move from competence to craftsmanship to mastery and artistry has several key components: projects in real-world contexts and settings, work with expert practitioners, authentic applications of technological tools, and assessment through performances that demonstrate skill and understanding. To get at the core of this instructional approach, we need to describe the kind of learning process we strive for in our schools.

# LEARNING IN THE FUNNEL

Roger Martin (2009) uses the metaphor of a "knowledge funnel" to describe how successful businesses provide products and services to their customers. Businesses (we would include all manner of entrepreneurs and tinkerers), he observes, are successful when they can work within an area that has a lot of unknowns ("mysteries"); develop strategies and tactics ("heuristics") for understanding and resolving those unknowns and challenges; develop efficient, often formulaic, responses ("algorithms") to those challenges; and eventually convert those responses into automatic behavior that increases productivity and effectiveness. They hone these algorithms (a formula or recipe, a set of instructions, a step-by-step procedure) to achieve increased efficiencies, look for more mysteries to solve, and repeat the cycle. They find mysteries by listening to their customers and then begin working along the funnel/value chain. We think a "learning funnel" (see figure below) is precisely what schools need to employ when designing engaging learning opportunities for their students (Washor and Mojkowski 2011a, 2011b).

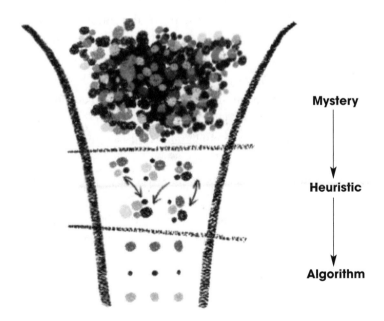

Mystery

Heuristic

Algorithm

Starting with a student's interests is most important in addressing both the Common Core and the uncommon core standards. Deep and rigorous learning involves a back-and-forth progression—linear and nonlinear—from mystery through heuristics and algorithms to codes (digital or not). Learning begins when the learner encounters something she or he wishes to learn. At first, there are lots of unknowns: *How does that work? How can I learn to do that?*

Bill Strickland, a MacArthur fellow and founder and CEO of Manchester Bidwell Corporation, in Pittsburgh, tells how he was introduced to pottery and art:

> It started back in 1965, at Oliver High School in the Manchester neighborhood of Pittsburgh. I was a young kid just about flunking out of school, and one afternoon I happened to walk past the ceramics studio. I glanced inside and here was this man throwing pots. Frank Ross. A Wednesday afternoon. Now, I don't know how many of you have ever seen a ceramics wheel turning, but if you have, you know it's magic. It was like a big invisible hand lifted me up and carried me over to that wheel. (Brant 2005)

Strickland was at the sweet spot in the learning funnel, eager to learn the tacit as well as the explicit, to observe and probe the subtle understanding that leads to craftsmanship, mastery, and artistry. *Can you teach me the techniques for throwing the clay? Can you show me how you hold your hands to achieve that special shape?*

Students, working within their interests, want to make sense of mysteries regarding those interests. They want to learn how to think about those mysteries, how to solve the challenges that the mysteries present. This requires that they develop and use heuristics, what teachers might call problem-finding and problem-solving strategies, the basic tools for figuring things out.

As learners discover, create, and employ heuristics, they also create algorithms that allow them to learn and perform more efficiently and automatically (Benjamin Bloom [1986] calls this "automaticity"). Algorithms help learners put some skills on automatic pilot so that they have more time to investigate more mysteries.

For young people learning outside school (when the teacher isn't watching, if you will), this process plays out in any number of ways. Imagine Rachel, for example, observing the ways that design firms develop their product ideas, at first mimicking their methods and ultimately developing some of her own. Observe her joining a community of young designers on the Internet to share challenges, debate the merits of various heuristics, and exchange a few well-tested methods.

This is the journey of deep, funneled learning students need, and they need to experience this journey over and over again throughout their K–12 education, each time getting more sophisticated at discovering mysteries, experimenting with strategies for solving those mysteries, and creating algorithms. Learning and using algorithms do not constitute deep learning, but creating and understanding them most certainly do.

When schools spend most of their time with students on algorithms they do not understand, students get lost—sadly, however, not lost in the funnel but lost in the jumble of facts, formulas, and rules they did not create. The result is confusion followed by disengagement.

The learning funnel is a useful tool for thinking about learning in a variety of contexts and settings outside school. Anyone doing work that requires improvising and then incorporating discoveries into repeatable processes is using the funnel. Highly creative people—those most valued in current and emerging workplaces and communities—view play, improvisation, and discovery as part of their work. Many of these repeatable processes, these algorithms, are tacit and not so easily passed from one learner to another. But teachers with great coaching skills can address tacit learning through demonstrations, modeling, and coaching. They can model how to employ heuristics in dealing with the real-world constraints that occur in most projects—for example, when a chef must adjust a recipe because an ingredient is missing or a diner has a food allergy or when an architect must adapt her designs to a new location or a reduced budget. It's not just jazz musicians who need to learn how to improvise. The yin and yang of play and practice are essential in all careers and therefore essential to learning and working in the funnel.

In *Every Patient Tells a Story: Medical Mysteries and the Art of Diagnosis* (2009), author and doctor Lisa Sanders uses stories to illustrate the way doctors move from mysteries and heuristics to algorithms. The popular television program, *House M.D.*, employed Sanders as a consultant to help design the episodes that, each week, showed the practice of medicine advancing through the learning funnel.

Here's a true story of a learner in the funnel. Late in 2010, thirteen-year-old Aidan Dwyer (2011) reported on a personal science experiment that caused quite a stir. His "discovery" of a more efficient array of solar panels won him a national science competition award and widespread recognition for his idea. That recognition prompted a closer examination of his reasoning and calculations by the scientific community, which revealed that he had measured the wrong thing, rendering his findings incorrect. The Internet lit up, as many in and outside the scientific community commented—some roughly—on his mistake. Aidan, a true learner, returned to his pursuits to understand the origins of his error and renew his studies. As we write, Aiden is still working the funnel, trying out a few more heuristics and tweaking his algorithms. He will no doubt continue to receive critiques from experts as he continues his work.

We think Wynton Marsalis (2008), a renowned teacher, would be pleased with Aidan's approach to science. "The best musicians know this music isn't about 'schools' at all," Marsalis has observed. "What is true about what musicians know is true in all fields and endeavors. Like my father says, 'There's only one school, the school of, "Can you play?"'" Aidan can play.

We would like to report that Aidan did all his research as part of his school-based learning, but there is no evidence that the school played much of a role. Often, young people need to pursue their learning funnels outside school, because the school controls nearly every aspect of a project, from the questions students might address to how the project is framed and conducted to how credit is awarded for answers and outcomes. How would a traditional school have assessed Aiden's "failure" to find the correct solution to the problem he identified and attempted to solve? Would it have awarded him credit for his question and his insightful heuristics, or would it have focused solely on his incorrect algorithm?

A passion for rocketry motivated Homer "Sonny" Hickam Jr., the "rocket boy" in the movie *October Sky* (Johnston 1999), to learn high-level math, but when he brought that learning into school, he was accused of cheating. The school had no way of paying attention to his out-of-school learning.

# PRODUCTIVE PROJECTS

Projects—small and large, individual and group—are a staple of our instructional design. Given Big Picture's focus on personalized learning, the majority of project work is individualized but nested within a community of practice. The learning funnel helps us see how to design projects to support productive learning:

- Projects originate in mystery as complex problems in real-world contexts and settings related to the student's interests and curiosities. Prepackaged projects will not do.

- Project work takes place in authentic contexts and settings.

- Time must be variable, allowing opportunities to go deep, even to double back and pursue related problems (more mysteries) as the need arises.

- Projects require the use of multiple strategies (heuristics).

- Project work, products as well as performance, is evaluated by adults doing similar work in businesses and the community.

- Projects lead to the development of algorithms that can be applied in future learning.

- Students—together with their teachers—assess their own projects and plan their future learning.

Great projects employ the learning funnel design, challenging students to discover mysteries and unknowns, craft strategies for understanding and solving those mysteries, and developing procedures for addressing similar problems. This approach gives students experience in creating, inventing, discovering, and applying rules of engagement in solving problems, necessary learning outcomes that can be accomplished only by starting students at the mystery end of the learning funnel and supporting them as they work their way through.

Focusing on algorithms may work well when learning/using the alphabet or the multiplication table but is minimally helpful in working through real-world problems and projects that require complex thinking. Competence in merely *using* algorithms is likely not good enough to negotiate life's problems or obtain high-paying work. Such work requires competence—we might say *craftsmanship*—in employing sophisticated heuristics to address challenging mysteries. Algorithmic jobs are typically the low-wage kind that get automated or outsourced.

THE BEST TEACHERS EMPLOY A RANGE OF STRATEGIES FOR BRINGING INCREASED RIGOR TO STUDENTS' PROJECTS . . . AND ENGAGE STUDENTS AROUND THEIR INTERESTS . . .

The best teachers employ a range of strategies for bringing increased rigor to students' projects. They engage students around their interests and start with the essential elements of rigor—complexity, breadth and depth, connections, and multiple disciplines (including reading and understanding relevant literature). They help students encounter the uncertainty and complexity of real-world projects and learn how the real world operationally defines rigor. Students observe adults doing rigorous work and, through in-depth reading, connect to the knowledge and skills nested within and across disciplines.

Teachers can use projects to help students develop their problem-solving strategies. For example, they can introduce changes and constraints or bring in expert practitioners to discuss real-world challenges for which no perfect solutions are possible. Students learn how to improvise not only to demonstrate their artistry, as jazz musicians do, but also out of necessity.

Teachers can help students find and communicate with adults and other students who are working on similar interests and projects. Students learn how to engage these adults in serious conversations about their work and observe how they do that work. What kind of problems do the adults confront? How do they go about solving them? How do they network with others working on similar problems?

Teachers also help students understand and pursue relationships between their projects and other disciplines. They help students form communities of practice around the project, some based within the school and others based in the community, including the virtual community, outside school.

Great teachers employ assessment criteria and processes that accommodate the complexity of rigorous student learning, including the processes and techniques the student employs. Actual performances (in school or in the workplace), exhibitions, project reports, and narrative assessments are the primary vehicles for assessing the depth, breadth, and quality of student learning, particularly learning over time.

Teachers can also make the projects more complex, make the tasks more challenging, requiring increasingly more sophisticated work (processes and techniques as well as products) and thereby pushing each student to the edge of his or her competence and enabling an extraordinary breadth and depth of learning. Nel Noddings, Stanford University professor and author of *The Challenge to Care in Schools* (2005), reminds us that such breadth and depth require large investments of flexible time for play and practice.

Project-based learning, if well designed and executed, is a compelling avenue for learning. Projects provide opportunities to pursue a single topic, issue, or challenge over time and in depth. The potential for craftsmanship is built in, as is the demand for drawing deeply on multidisciplinary competencies. The use of our senses—and our sensibilities—comes into play. Kyna Leski (2012) sees sensibility—keen intellectual perception—as the cusp between percept and concept.

A project developed by one of our students illustrates how Big Picture Learning schools address the project design standards we listed earlier.

From the time he was a young boy, Huber was interested in maps, places, and his community. While at the Big Picture Learning school in Oakland, he traveled to Chile and Thailand and observed the changes taking place in those countries. On his return, Huber decided that he wanted to bring about some changes in his community. Through his internship in a mayoral election campaign, he noticed a relationship between voting behavior and home ownership: people who did not own homes were more likely not to vote. Huber reasoned that one cause of this was their sense that their voices would not be heard.

Based on his work and his thinking about that work, Huber developed a senior project to address the problem he identified. He organized a seminar about purchasing a home. He focused the project specifically on teachers in Oakland because he felt indebted to them and because teachers—like so many others—are routinely shut out of Oakland's high-priced housing market. He began the project with an internship at a real estate agency to learn about the housing market and more specifically about low-income housing programs.

Huber organized the seminar with the help of his teacher-advisor and his mentor at the real estate agency. He invited presenters from real estate companies, community organizations, banks, and city and state agencies. He also invited two teachers who had successfully bought homes in the Bay Area to speak. The symposium was a success. About twenty-five teachers attended and several began actively searching for homes.

Upon graduation, Huber went to UC Berkeley using scholarships from the Bill and Melinda Gates Foundation and the Rainbow Push Coalition. He took with him his deep interest in his community:

> I just want to be there at UC Berkeley and study political science.
> After I graduate from college, which is hopefully going to be four years
> from now, I want to come back prepared with more resources or better
> background and a better sense of *how* I can serve my community. . . .
> I think that's one of the questions that I'm going to be asking for the
> next four years or even a lifetime—how I can help the community I
> grew up in?

Technology applications play an important role in our view of productive learning through projects. We are not concerned here about online learning systems for skills development, although our schools strive to use these systems appropriately. Instead, our focus is on how students learn to use technology tools as expert practitioners in their areas of interest use them in the real world. How, for example, do chefs, architects, farmers, and expert practitioners in every profession use technology to be more effective and efficient and to achieve craftsmanship, mastery, and artistry in their performance? Big Picture Learning schools require students to seek out answers to these questions and to use those answers to guide their own applications of technology.

It is true that many young people are technologically savvy, but often their skills and understanding are focused on such tools as Facebook and Twitter. Far fewer students are even familiar, much less skilled, with the technology tools used in the careers they wish to pursue. That is the focus that great teachers employ in helping students design and implement their projects.

# HOW DO WE KNOW WHAT'S BEEN LEARNED?

Our view of learning opportunities and environments provokes the question of how schools should assess the learning we have described. A few key points are worth emphasizing.

First, the focus of current school assessments is dangerously myopic, fixated as they are on a narrow band of competencies. Schools need to bring what is currently on the periphery—arts and design, creativity and invention, career skills and personal competencies—into the center of their teaching and assessment focus. Schools are often unaware of what students can do in these much-neglected areas of the curriculum, but they add important value in the schools' quest to prepare young people for success.

Second, the type of assessment used is similarly constricted, principally the paper-and-pencil test. A substantial percentage of high-stakes tests employ mostly or exclusively a multiple-choice format (Darling-Hammond 2011, Fairtest.org 2007). These tests are as unauthentic as the learning they are designed to assess. Should we complain about such a perfect match? Yes! Noddings (2005) adds another caution: the pressure of standardized testing is decreasing the time teachers and students have to "explore topics of interest more deeply." Complaints are coming from students, parents, teachers, and principals.

Schools need to add to paper-and-pencil tests a range of assessments that use performances—demonstrations and products—in real-world settings and contexts to judge skill and understanding. Further, they need to vastly expand the use of student self-assessments that teach while they test. The essence of accountability is that students are able to describe their efforts and accomplishments—formulate their learning first for themselves and then for others. The most effective accountability emanates within the individual. In our schools, advisors regularly engage their students in self-assessment, asking such questions as *how do you think you did?* and *what do you have to learn next?* The resulting dialogue can be a powerful learning experience. External accountability methods and measures, however important for valid and reliable judgments, are likely to meet with substantial resistance unless there is a better balance with internal, capacity-building accountability.

Finally, schools need to help students prepare portfolios of their work that show, in many formats, their general and specific competencies and how they are ready to apply these competencies to the work they wish to do. Rachel used a range and depth of information to document her readiness for the work she wished to do. Like an accomplished Girl Scout, she had certificates as evidence of her competence and provided artifacts and videos to demonstrate her accomplishments. With "only" a technical college degree, how do you think she would have fared in the interview if she had relied on a traditional transcript?

What if schools were able to create new credentials that are based on demonstrations of skills and understanding and that recognize in some formal way skills and understanding developed in any setting? What if employers got serious about looking beyond a high school diploma or undergraduate degree to focus on competence as measured by actual performances that demonstrate skill and understanding?

# NEW WINE IN NEW BOTTLES

We've provided, in a rather large nutshell, our answers to those three important questions regarding learning. Admittedly, this is a highly condensed version of our view of productive learning, but we have tried to make the key principles, features, and components clear:

- Schools need to employ a broader and deeper definition of what constitutes success, one that embraces the many ways that young people engage with, understand, and make their way in the world.

- Schools must allow students to address learning standards through their interests and encourage variation in performances and products that demonstrate learning.

- Schools must give increased attention to creativity and invention throughout the curriculum.

- Schools must push students to the edge of their competence in a quest for craftsmanship, mastery, and artistry.

- Schools must help students undertake complex projects based on questions with no easy solutions nested in real-world settings and contexts.

- Schools should provide students with many opportunities and ways to show what they know and can do.

- Schools should help students learn to use technology as it is employed by professionals doing the work the students wish to do.

Each of these principles, features, and components is significant individually; their combination constitutes a substantial and significant challenge to prevailing practice in most schools. Yet such learning abounds outside school. For an example, visit the website of New York's Museum of Natural History and read about the young scholars whose work is documented there. These students, typically working outside their school's instructional program, identified their own questions and problems, undertook their own explorations, made their own discoveries, and produced their own reports and products. Adults supported them in their work, but it is unclear what their schools did to support their learning other than sign off on their projects and continue to provide the standard curriculum. The students' projects were not schoolwork, *but they could have been.* They were probably the most authentic and enduring parts of these students' learning.

In conclusion, read this story of an unconventional learner and think about how schools could embrace such learning.

Sean Collins, a world-renowned surfer, died in 2011 (Borte and Surfline 2012). His was not a household name like some of the famous dropouts we have cited, but his story illuminates the way that productive learning can be accomplished outside school. Indeed, Sean's story reminds us of Ray Charles' observation, "I always wanted to be great. I never wanted to be famous."

Collins was raised in Southern California, and his love of the ocean was formed aboard his father's fifty-foot sailboat, first venturing around Long Beach and then entering races to Mexico and Hawaii. He began surfing when he was eight: "I was always looking at charts to plan my surfing and sailing, and developed a keen sense about the ocean, which is at the core of what I live for today."

After his graduation from Long Beach's Wilson High School, where he skipped many classes to go surfing, Collins attended Long Beach City College but dropped out after two years. He received no formal training beyond a couple of courses in meteorology. He worked as a waiter and bartender so he could continue to surf, chase waves, and study weather charts to predict future swells (sounds like heuristics to us). Weather faxes from New Zealand via a shortwave radio allowed him to compare these week-old charts with the surf behind his Seal Beach home. He scoured the National Weather Service Library in Los Angeles and eventually devised his own formulas (might we call them algorithms?) for forecasting swells. "People started calling," he reflected. " 'You don't know me,' they'd say. 'I'm a friend of a friend, but what do you think Mexico's gonna be like next week?'"

In 1984, Collins began offering surf reporting and forecasting services to Surfline, a phone service started by some Orange County businessmen. After two years he left to begin Wavetrak, a rival company that was so successful he could afford to buy out Surfline in 1990. His success continued with other products and services: WaveFax, a subscription-based service; Surfline.com, a site with free surf reports from around the country; and Surfcam, the precedent for live-camera surf images.

Collins left school to pursue his learning. He developed and implemented his learning plan, school playing no more than a bit part in his learning journey. Over time he identified the important competencies, worked his way through the learning funnel, and created heuristics and algorithms that set standards for craftsmanship, mastery, and artistry. His schools might have added value to his work if they had had a leaving-to-learn program. Just how they might have done that is our next focus.

# LEAVING TO LEARN

We have shared stories of many people who left school to learn things their schools would not or could not help them learn. How might schools have kept Les Paul, Whoopi Goldberg, and James Cameron (as well as the many young people we have talked about) in their classrooms, pursuing productive learning? We find our answer in the words of our colleague and jazz musician John Anter: "I got to go so I can come back."

Schools need to let students leave—leave to learn, that is—and provide ways for them to bring their learning and accomplishments back to school and make them part of their programs of study. Then, as the directions on the shampoo bottle advise, *repeat*, throughout each student's entire school experience.

Learning does not stop when a student leaves school. It often continues in a different form and with a different focus. Perhaps it's on a job or in private study or while pursuing a hobby. Leaving-to-learn programs allow students to pursue productive learning in settings and contexts—businesses, community organizations, government and nonprofit agencies, travel—schools cannot provide. Learning outside school often addresses students' expectations and "the deeper four" more than school-based learning does.

The next two chapters describe the kind of leaving-to-learn *opportunities* and environments schools need to provide

TO KEEP ALL THEIR STUDENTS LEARNING PRODUCTIVELY. THEY INCLUDE MORE NUTS-AND-BOLTS EXPLANATIONS AND ADDRESS THE PRAGMATIC ASPECTS OF OUR APPROACH, INCLUDING A FEW COMMON SENSE "RULES OF THE ROAD."

THERE ARE ALSO SOME BASIC TOOLS—PURPOSE STATEMENTS, PLANS, ORGANIZATIONS, MENTORS, AND PORTFOLIOS—LEARNERS WILL NEED TO GET THE MOST OUT OF LEAVING. SCHOOLS CAN USE THESE SAME TOOLS TO ENGAGE A SECOND GROUP OF YOUNG PEOPLE: THOSE WHO LEFT SCHOOL AND WISH TO RETURN AND PICK UP WHERE THEY LEFT OFF BUT IN A NEW AND BETTER WAY.

SETTING UP AND MAINTAINING LEAVING-TO-LEARN PROGRAMS THAT SERVE EVERY HIGH SCHOOL STUDENT IS A CHALLENGE, AND WE NEED TO CHANGE THE ASPECTS OF SCHOOL THAT IMPEDE OUR DOING SO. WHAT PARTS OF THE WAY THAT EDUCATION IS CURRENTLY STRUCTURED NEED TO BE MODIFIED TO SUPPORT PRODUCTIVE LEARNING? WHAT POLICIES AND REGULATIONS REGARDING TEACHERS AND MENTORS NEED TO CHANGE? WE SUGGEST ANSWERS TO THESE AND OTHER QUESTIONS BUT RECOGNIZE THAT EACH SCHOOL NEEDS TO CREATE ITS OWN. EACH SCHOOL NEEDS TO LEARN AND WORK WITHIN ITS OWN LEARNING FUNNEL.

Chapter

# 7

# WAYS TO LEAVE FOR LEARNING

*A child educated only at school is an uneducated child.*

—GEORGE SANTAYANA

Bored in school, Carol left her California high school in 1981 to work as a senate page. When her term ended, she moved with her family to Florida. She found the schools there just as boring as those she left. For one of her projects, she wanted to take a delegation of twenty-five students from five different continents to India. The school refused to approve the necessary time off, so Carol quit and went anyway.

A few months later, she went to Mexico City to study Spanish and work at Amnesty International. She returned in 1983, enrolled in a Florida high school, and was accepted to Yale. However, the high school wouldn't give her a diploma because she didn't have the proper number of credits. She convinced them to at least give her a vocational diploma and went off to Yale, probably the only student ever to have been accepted there with that credential. In 2003, she was invited to return to her California school to give the commencement address and receive a college prep diploma.

While Carol is not a typical dropout and her story is unusual, we hope it presages how many if not most students' learning journeys may look in the not-too-distant future. High school leaving-to-learn opportunities come in a range of shapes and sizes, from the typical field trip and guest speaker to the much more intensive internship, travel itinerary, paid or unpaid work, college or online course, special project, entrepreneurial venture, and gap year. They vary in duration, intensity, and the length of the "umbilical cord" between the student and the school.

If you think some high schools already do a bit of this or that, you're right—and wrong. Many schools do provide one or more of these opportunities, but typically the range is limited. Most out-of-school learning programs do not address the following criteria, which are essential to a high-quality leaving-to-learn program:

- They are open to all students in all grades.

- They are an integral part of students' learning trajectory, seamlessly merging in-school and out-of-school learning.

- They address important learning standards (academic, workplace, and personal).

- They complement and supplement the in-school experience, providing productive learning experiences that students cannot get in school.

- They address students' expectations.

- They contribute to productive learning as we have defined it.

- They are awarded academic and graduation credit.

The first criterion is very important. Leaving-to-learn opportunities are not a reward for students who do well in school. They are essential for all students so that many more students will excel. To that end, they address students' expectations in ways that traditional schools cannot address well or at all. However, schools who offer out-of-school learning-to-leave experiences can claim them as their own.

Many of these opportunities also place students at the side of adults who share their interests, which provides substantial and significant benefits. Young people learn to behave properly by hanging around with adults, often without anyone realizing the behavior is being learned. If students act immaturely or irresponsibly in an out-of-school setting, they will be ignored or asked to leave. There are consequences for behaving poorly. Young people understand this and are eager to act like adults in settings and contexts they choose for their learning. Also, students build social capital by developing relationships with adults who have similar interests; they have a network for finding future work.

The case for leaving-to-learn opportunities is compelling. If we accept students' expectations as requirements in designing schools, particularly high schools, then leaving-to-learn opportunities are a critical component. The range of leaving-to-learn opportunities can provide every learner some form of out-of-school learning.

# LEAVING-TO-LEARN OPPORTUNITIES

## EXPERTS-IN-RESIDENCE

A rich array of community experts—artists, scientists, entrepreneurs, performers—can work alongside teachers to bring the outside world into school projects (disciplinary and multidisciplinary) and the learning associated with them. The school might provide space in which these specialists can work so students get to observe a slice of the real world. Experts-in-residence constitute a kind of leaving, in that students are working with people who bring the workplace and the community into the classroom and after-school programs.

Most often, experts-in-residence are career professionals or community artists. At the Met school in Providence, Rhode Island, local performing artists work with several students on a variety of projects in exchange for being able to use the school's black box theater after hours and on weekends. Brian Mills, the Met's director of media and performing arts, describes a typical partnership:

> We worked with the All Children's Theatre and became their home theatre in return for mentoring Met students. The company's artistic director and producers helped Met students create their own theatre company, Dynamic Theatre. Students produced performances they wrote themselves, as well as performed classics and adaptations of screenplays. They raised funds for their productions and ended each

season with enough money to purchase the props and materials for their next season.

Also at the Met, Bill Daugherty, a former vice president of the National Basketball Association, established the country's first Center for Innovation and Entrepreneurship on a high school campus. Daugherty brings in business and community experts to help budding student entrepreneurs design and launch businesses that move out into the community.

An interesting variation on in-school spaces for experts-in-residence is the makerspace:

> Modeled after hackerspaces, a makerspace is a place where young people have an opportunity to explore their own interests, learn to use tools and materials, and develop creative projects. It could be embedded inside an existing organization or stand alone on its own. It could be a simple room in a building or an outbuilding that's closer to a shed. The key is that it can adapt to a wide variety of uses and can be shaped by educational purposes as well as the students' creative goals. (Makerspacc 2012)

Establishing a makerspace in a school is an excellent way to attract local artisans, designers, craftsmen, and tinkerers to work with students as models, coaches, and mentors. The space might operate on weekends and be open to all "makers" in the community.

Anthony, a student in a Big Picture Learning school in Newark, New Jersey, defines industrial design as "when you see something and you know that it needs something to enhance it, and you make it, limited only by your imagination." He was one of the first students to apply for an internship at an exploratory industrial design workshop at the local museum. He says:

> I am interested in making things, from music to film to art. I am always looking forward to doing things, building things, making things. Since I have been in the program I have been creating stuff. It is a lot of fun. I entered the program because I wanted to do something different but found that it was a really cool program. I made a video game controller and joystick using Makerbot. I made a video game using Scratch. I made

a T-shirt using a vinyl cutter and paint. I made a house using a vinyl cutter. I made and programmed an arduino board, which is like the brain of a machine—it controls the machine. Mine reacted to my controller, blinked lights, and controlled an airplane.

In addition to the experience of building things, Anthony has connected with experts in the field of engineering and industrial design whom he believes will help him in the future. His hard work culminated with a presentation at the World Science and Arts Festival in New York City; an article in the local newspaper; and a visit from Newark's mayor, Cory Booker. Anthony has aspirations to be either an industrial designer or a multimedia producer.

## ROAD TRIPS

Road trips are great ways for students to observe what's going on in the community or in a workplace. Students conduct interviews, people-watch, and otherwise interact with people, places, and things. Roadtrip Nation (RTN) (www.roadtripnation.com), a website that helps students meet people who are doing things the students are interested in, has developed a curriculum schools use to engage students in challenging projects and provide credit for learning accomplished out on the road.

Antonia Slagle, an advisor at the Big Picture Learning school in Sacramento, used the Roadtrip Nation curriculum for an entire school year as part of a life exploration program. "We did activities once a week, which culminated in students conducting their own RTN interviews, which they posted on the RTN page." The Roadtrip Nation experience allowed Slagle's students to confront the real-world demands of their desired careers while receiving academic credit for their learning. "Watching interviews with famous or established individuals," Slagle noted, "students could see that fame doesn't just happen. It is the effect of an incredible tenacity. Also, students gained a better understanding of how they could explore their communities to identify individuals who shared their passions. One way they achieved this was to research local experts and seek them out for interviews."

## AFTER-SCHOOL PROGRAMS

This category includes a wide variety of learning opportunities: clubs (chess, photography), projects (newspaper, yearbook), and competitions (math, robotics). These programs may be offered in or outside school and may be conducted by school faculty or by nonschool, community-based organizations. Many schools already offer after-school programs, but very few align the learning taking place in these programs with the formal, in-school curriculum and award academic and graduation credit. After-school programs are an integral part of leaving-to-learn programs.

The Sol Collective (www.wix.com/solcollective/sol-collective), a Sacramento community-based partnership whose mission is to use art, education, and technology to mobilize and empower the community, aligns its work with students with their school learning. Many students at the Met school in Sacramento are at the Collective during the school day taking part in internships, workshops, and service learning projects in such fields as permaculture, digital technology, graphic design, and music and video production; most continue their work after school. Many students design and market entrepreneurial projects geared to improving their community. Their learning receives academic and graduation credit.

Estella Sanchez, executive director and founder of the Sol Collective and a former adviser at the Sacramento Met school, describes how the collective's after-school programs address community needs and integrate with students' school learning:

> At Sol Collective students have either enhanced our existing programs or developed projects based on needs they saw in the community. As mentors we provide resources and guidance in order for students to implement their projects successfully. Many of the students' projects have influenced or become current programs.
>
> Ruby's interest in sustainable living in her low-income neighborhood led her to organize cross-cultural youth meetings at Sol Collective. She researched various topics, gave brief presentations on them, and then gave her peers the opportunity to dialogue. One evening after a lively discussion about the lack of access to healthy food in their community, Ruby decided to learn to grow her own food. She co-led a

group of students and community members in building a small garden in a gravel alley, using sheet mulching. By summer she was a youth advisor to the city's green steering committee. The program she initiated is now part of a ten-year, multiagency effort to build healthier communities in ten California cities impacted by poverty. (Sanchez 2012)

## COMMUNITY SERVICE

Most young people are eager to learn and work in their communities. Remember Huber, whose home-ownership project in Oakland (see Chapter 6) prompted the teachers in his school to buy homes in nearby Oakland neighborhoods?

Many schools require community service as a graduation requirement. These projects are as varied as the communities. They also vary in duration and intensity, from a one-time effort to clean a neighborhood lot to designing a new playground to volunteering in the children's wing of the local hospital. Service projects are excellent opportunities to address core learning standards in a number of disciplines and develop academic, career, and personal competency.

For example, Huber's advisor helped him design his project to address California's state educations standards as well as the University of California's specific "a–g" (subject-area) requirements for admission.[1] A complex project like Huber's addresses language arts, social science, and mathematics competencies and, equally important, selected career and life competencies, such as problem solving, leadership, creative thinking, persistence, collaboration, empathy, and leadership.

Paul Hudak, an advisor at Terra Nova High School, in Beaverton, Oregon, developed a community service program that is part of the fabric of the school and its community. In 2008, Hudak converted an empty ball field at the high school into a place where students could learn how to run a farm. The school received a grant to prepare the land and create a community-supported agriculture program in which subscribers picked

---

1. See www.ucop.edu/agguide/ for University of California a–g subject-area requirements.

up a box of seasonal fruits and vegetables each week. Hudak spends his days educating students about agriculture, sustainability, and business through internships on the Terra Nova community farm. He was recognized for his achievements in 2011 (Fong 2012).

Community service helps students develop empathy for people in different and often challenging circumstances. True empathy is engendered through deep, broad, sustained interaction with the real world. Empathy so developed is more likely to be authentic, informed, and sustained; less an abstraction and more concrete; less reality TV or the evening news, where a twenty-second spot on starvation in Somalia deludes viewers into believing they understand all there is to understand about the tragedy. Authentic empathy is the lifeblood of successful entrepreneurism.

For schools to help their students develop empathy through community service and related work, the schools themselves need to demonstrate empathy for their students by delivering on students' expectations. Students want their teachers to know them well and to use that knowledge to guide their learning.

## INTERNSHIPS/APPRENTICESHIPS

Internships are increasingly popular ways of providing leaving-to-learn opportunities. They include a broad and diverse range of activities, from job shadowing to semester and yearlong positions in a business or the community. Typically these internships are unpaid; some lead to certificates that document achievement of certain standards of competence in a skill; others may lead to paid internships or a full-time job.

Although most educators think of internships as appropriate for the "vocational" student—particularly those not going on to a four-year college—we view internships as an essential learning experience for all students. There is or certainly should be a "career" and a "technical" aspect to all learning, just as there is or should be an applied, "hands-on" aspect to all learning. Can you imagine high school students aspiring to be architects, designers, doctors, or lawyers who would not want to learn firsthand what the career entails and what they need to learn to enter it?

Jake, a student in the Big Picture Learning school in Newport, Rhode Island, reflects on his internship: "Learning by doing and learning by reading—those are two of my main things. It's a point of contention between me and teachers in general, because I feel as though I can teach myself almost anything." Jake designed and manufactured his own trawl fishing nets during his internship. His advisor supported him by incorporating relevant academic, career, and life competencies into the internship. Jake honed his craft and now is a professional fisherman working in the Alaskan pollack fishing industry.

As Mike Rose reminds us, all work offers robust challenges, and internships are no exception. In *The Mind at Work: Valuing the Intelligence of the American Worker* (2004) he states:

> We mistake narrowness for rigor, but actually we are not rigorous enough. To acknowledge our collective capacity is to take the concept of variability seriously. Not as slots along a simplified cognitive continuum or as a neat high-low distribution, but as a bountiful and layered field, where many processes and domains of knowledge interact. Such a model demands more not less from those of us who teach, or who organize work, or who develop social policy. To affirm this conception of mind and work is to be vigilant for the intelligence not only in the boardroom but on the shop floor; in the laboratory and alongside the house frame; in the classroom, the garage, the busy restaurant, vibrant with desire and strategic movement. This is a model of mind that befits the democratic imagination. (216)

## COLLEGE COURSES

Many high schools provide opportunities for students to take one or more college courses. Most of these are conducted at the high school, but sometimes the high school students take the course on the college campus along with college students, which provides a richer experience.

Nearly every Big Picture Learning school offers this option; the Met in Providence initiated the practice in 1995. Many students earn up to two years of college classes before finishing high school. While we are surprised when our students eagerly sit through hour-long lectures with little or no professor-student interaction, we know the students are doing it by choice and that it reduces the number of courses they'll need to take when they go to college. Taking a college course also shows students they can learn on the college level in a college environment, no small accomplishment for a student who is often the first member of the family planning to attend college.

A Met student in Sacramento used the school's partnership with the local community college ("the panther pipeline") to achieve her dream of becoming a dental hygienist. The school helped her arrange an internship at a dentist's office, enroll in HCD 310 (a course on how to be a better student), and get counseling about available programs. The student is now taking Introduction to Allied Health Occupations and will be a full-time student at Sacramento Community College in the fall.

Josh, a student at MetWest High School, in Oakland, is an example of how the partnerships high schools form with postsecondary institutions can serve each student's individual—and sometimes exceptional—interests and talents. Josh and his parents chose MetWest because its unique educational program offered what they thought he needed. A small, safe, nurturing community, the school was able to respond to and support Josh's social skill development as a person with Asperger syndrome through its partnership with the local community college.

Josh took advanced courses at the college and took advantage of MetWest's internship program to learn how his interests might play out in the adult world of work. As a shy ninth grader, he interned at a social justice nonprofit dedicated to educating high school students about the risks and benefits of enrolling in the military. While the exhibitions he presented in ninth grade were detailed and chock-full of information, he was barely audible and rarely raised his head or made eye contact. In his junior year, Josh enrolled in an advanced literature seminar, began to develop friendships with his classmates, and joined two other boys in the class to train for and then run the Los Angeles marathon. For a student who had always been physically awkward and avoided physical and group activity, this was a watershed experience.

In eleventh grade Josh also began an internship at the California Academy of Sciences. During his last two years of high school, he spent two full days a week there looking at, learning about, classifying, and labeling mollusks. He and his mentor worked for long stretches in engrossed silence, occasionally conversing about the mollusks, other marine biology topics, or politics. He sometimes spent full days alone with the mollusks, speaking to no one. He found joy and fulfillment in a small windowless room surrounded by mollusks, happy as a clam!

Josh's dream was to attend Oxford University. Armed with more than two years of college credit, real-world work experience at a nationally renowned institution, and the social skills and confidence to navigate a new city and university system, he headed off to Oxford two months after graduating. Josh has just completed his first year at Oxford, and his confidence, joy, and connections have continued to grow and develop.

With a robust leaving-to-learn program, schools not only can offer college-level experiences to all their students but also can customize this college experience to students' interests and talents. The result is a few valuable college credits and, more important, a deep engagement in learning.

## WORK

Many students need to work to help support their family or earn spending money. Some students start their own businesses outside school. Most schools think it is unusual for high school students to find work aligned with their learning, but we are convinced that most work, even the most varied—helping out at the family business, sales, technology support, skilled labor, baby sitting, waiting tables—can be matched with academic, career, and personal competencies. Good work, as described by Howard Gardner, Mihaly Csikszentmihalyi, and William Damon (2001) in a book with that title, is essential for developing social and intellectual competence.

Work comes in many forms, and few schools consider it part of students' learning. If teachers and administrators are willing to look, however, they will find that their working students are developing valuable career and personal competencies that are difficult to teach or assess in school. Met school student Michael turned the knowledge he gained during an internship at a technology company into a part-time job at a worldwide computer firm. Through that work, he was able to build a support network of adult mentors who had and continue to have a stake in his success. The social capital Michael developed (an important career and personal competency) helped him land a full-time job, gain certifications in technology, and continue his learning at a community college and then a local university. What better place than the workplace for developing career competencies!

Another student, Josh, rotated through a few internships before landing one with a local dance and theater company, where he discovered a calling as a hip-hop and break-dancer. While honing his dancing skills to a professional level, he became a skilled martial artist and adopted a healthy lifestyle of exercise, rest, and a vegetarian diet. Josh also discovered he had a head for business and decided to combine the two interests by getting a postsecondary degree in finance and promoting dance tours throughout the country. Since graduation, Josh has performed on over a thousand stages around the world, choreographed dances for Las Vegas performers, and learned nearly every aspect of the business aspects of performing. He continues to learn inside and outside his profession, recently receiving his FAA Airframe and Powerplant license. Josh was able to take the first steps on his unusual pathway to success through his internships.

## INDEPENDENT STUDY

This category includes individual projects focused on one or more disciplines but undertaken outside a regular academic course. Independent study can entail working with a tutor or coach and is sometimes combined with travel or an intensive, extended internship. For example, one of our students traveled to Japan to study the culture and learn the language. Another worked as an intern on a governor's commission for over a year. In each case, the teacher/advisor created a customized curriculum (including academic, career, and life competencies) around the independent study project.

We think of independent study as companies like Google and 3M do. Google, through its Time Off program, encourages its engineers to spend 20 percent of their time at work on projects that interest them (Mediratta and Bick 2007). Some of Google's newer services, such as Gmail, Google News, and AdSense, were developed through this program. 3M pioneered its 15 Percent Program in 1948 and required participating employees to share their off-the-books projects with their colleagues. The Post-it® Note may be the most famous of the products resulting from 3M's investment (Goetz 2011). What might students do if schools provided time to do this?

## TRAVEL

This isn't the traditional senior class trip to the big city, the trip with the family to visit relatives, or even family relocation. It is travel in which learning is intentionally embedded. It's often the best or only way to address specific learning objectives in a student's learning plan.

Travel is a difficult option for students with limited financial means, but schools and students can find ways to raise the necessary money. Big Picture Learning schools consider travel an integral part of students' curriculum and raise funds to support it.

Christsna transferred to MetWest, in Oakland, in his junior year, hoping to find a more personalized and caring environment in which his interests could become part of his high school education. Like many first-generation Cambodian Americans, Christsna knew few details of his family's experience during the Khmer Rouge years before they emigrated to the United States. Between his junior and senior year, Christsna traveled to Cambodia for the first time to explore his past; the trip was developed in connection with his advisor for school credit. He returned with his worldview expanded, his connections to both his cultures (Cambodian and American) deepened. During the trip he shot video for a documentary he intends to produce with the support of his mentor, a Cambodian American filmmaker at New American Media with whom he is interning. Supported by a Gates Millennium Scholarship, Christsna has begun his studies at UC Berkeley. (Christsna is also an accomplished spoken word poet and has been featured on HBO's *Brave New Voices*. Videos of him in performance can be viewed at www.youtube.com/watch?v=UDrabyySvEY, www.youtube.com/watch?v=qBxFtPpkdUE, and www.youtube.com/watch?v=jMB74_5BhrA.)

Travel can be an ideal setting—and provide the needed motivation—to pursue important learning. Yemell emigrated to the United States from Peru with his father and older brother at the age of twelve, leaving his younger brothers and mother in Lima. When he turned eighteen he was on his own. All through high school, he desperately wanted to drop out. His advisor at a Big Picture Learning school wanted to keep him in school and keep him engaged there. When he was a senior in high school he wanted to go back to Peru to see his mother and younger brothers for the first time in seven years and fulfill a childhood dream of seeing Machu Picchu, Cuzco, and the Nazca Lines. He sold his car and worked thirty hours a week at a local restaurant to fund his trip.

His advisor helped Yemell plan an itinerary, deal with logistics, and formulate what he hoped to gain from the trip. He researched ancient Incan culture and contemporary Peru for English language arts and history credit. While on his trip he continued to read, research, and write, sending weekly emails to his advisor. When he returned he presented an exhibition on Peru, also for academic credit. The trip was a life-changing experience. Some of the grief he carried subsided, and he seemed more at peace. Yemell eventually graduated college and is now a draftsman at an architecture firm. He also is exploring entrepreneurial ventures in Peru.

## GAP YEAR

Typically, gap years are taken between high school and college. However, a high school student can also take off a semester or a year to pursue alternative learning (which might include an extended internship or travel). Graham's story is an illustration of how school- and community-supported student learning can take place even after graduation.

Graham had been homeschooled his first three years of high school. He enrolled in a Big Picture Learning school for his senior year, arriving with some interesting passions: acting, soccer, alternative energy, photography, literature, and the French language. He was probably not as social as some of his peers, but as the year progressed he began to express himself through his passions and interests.

Graham worked intensively with a mentor who specialized in digital photography. He spent many hours learning the intricacies of his new digital camera so that he could become a better photographer. He highlighted his quarterly exhibitions with interesting photos he had taken, enthusiastically sharing the stories behind them.

Graham's family lives "off the grid," generating the electricity for their home through a combination of sun and wind, and throughout the year he interviewed and took photos of people in the community and their alternative energy projects. He talked with them about their backyard hydro projects, solar panels, and wind turbines. He presented his project to the community on senior project night and received high praise for his efforts.

Graham also wanted to improve his conversational French, but there weren't enough hours in the day to enroll in a college-level French program offered by a local college. However, after he graduated, Graham decided to take a year off before going to college. He wanted to spend some of that year in France improving his French. His family had lived there previously and had a few contacts. So he and a friend traveled to Europe. During the France leg of the journey, he worked in a family friend's vineyard and played soccer for a local club. While in Europe, Graham learned that he had been accepted to Bates College. The combination of homeschooling, traditional high school classes, college-level classes, internships, and a gap year readied Graham for his postsecondary learning.

## ENTREPRENEURIAL VENTURES

Confronted with diminished prospects for work in an anemic job market, many young people are eager to develop entrepreneurial competencies that will allow them to create their own jobs. These opportunities include business and social ventures, both for-profit and nonprofit.

Students at one Big Picture Learning school developed and marketed organic Big Picture Soda and sold it in several local stores, including a Whole Foods market. Local business leaders helped the students develop business and marketing plans, but the students made the decisions about products, packaging, placement, pricing, and distribution and made sales calls to the local markets. Their advisors made sure the students developed academic, career, and life skills as part of the venture. There was no need to cajole students into honing their writing and math competencies with so much motivation built right in.

At the Big Picture Film and Theater Arts Charter High School, in Los Angeles (www.bigpicturela.org), a team of students formed Urban Revolt Records, a company that won the Blastbeat World Finals Award for Music and Multimedia Companies, presented in Dublin. The Urban Revolt Records student team created a business plan for their company, identified and recruited talented young musicians in the area, promoted and staged concerts starring these groups, documented all their activities, and blogged about the project for the entire international Blastbeat community. The students also made formal presentations of their work at the Musicians' Institute in Hollywood. During the next school year, graduate students at the UCLA Anderson School of Management were mentors to the team, helping them refine and implement their business model and plan.

Empathy, which we mentioned earlier as an essential competency in community service, is equally important to entrepreneurs. It is no coincidence that the design thinking championed by IDEO, the design firm (www.ideo.com/expertise/play), and by the d.school, also known as the Hasso Plattner Institute of Design at Stanford (dschool.stanford.edu/blog/category/empathy/), includes empathy as a major component. Successful entrepreneurs typically are adept at getting inside the minds and hearts of their clients to best serve their needs and thereby reap success.

Adrian, a Native American graduate of our school in the Highline school district (near Seattle), is a social entrepreneur who credits his success to his empathy for the needs of students. Adrian works with the Native Student Alliance (NSA) and is a member of the Big Picture Native Wellness Team. He helps students with their coursework (preparing for exhibitions, for example), co-leads the weekly NSA meetings, and accompanies students on field trips. He has also been teaching an autobiography class and co-teaching the Native Games Curriculum.

Student Flavio came to the Met school in Providence, Rhode Island, after having been suspended several times in middle school and being thrown out of a private high school. At the Met, Flavio made it his mission to bring the taste of Peru to the world. Flavio comes from a family whose members own restaurants—his grandmother in Peru, his mother in Providence. Flavio studied the Hispanic market and identified a few products that showed promise. He participated in the Boston University Startup Weekend, a program typically populated by MBA students and degree-holders. He and a sixteen-year-old classmate, the only participants in a group of eighty who were under twenty-three years old, registered as a business partnership. They won third-place honors for their business concept and plan. The two also registered as a business partnership for Providence College's Startup Weekend and took third place as well.

## ONLINE LEARNING

The world of online learning includes coursework, mentoring, simulations, and affinity groups. Global communities address even the most unusual interests. Online learning can take place anytime, anywhere, in connection with both in-school and out-of-school learning. Students can produce as well as consume knowledge in these digital learning environments.

Dave Master, founder and director of ACME Animation, is a prototypical example of the power of online learning. Master, a world-class educator and former director of artist development at Warner Bros. Animation, developed an online service for schools through which graphics students have their work critiqued by professional animators. The online network is a virtual "experts-in-residence" program open to all interested students.

Many of these students eventually obtain high-paying jobs in the animation industry.

But ACME Animation is much more than a farm league for future
professional animators. In Master's words:

> We use animation to engage students as young as sixth grade in the
> arts. Most of the ACME students are middle and high school students
> in underserved communities. I think the reason many people think of
> us as a college animation program is because that is who the profes-
> sional artists mentor online. But ACME employs a *pay-it-forward* type
> system where pros mentor college students online, yet the college stu-
> dents *earn* that professional feedback by mentoring scores of middle
> and high school kids across the country.
>
> In effect, we've created a sort of Peace Corps of college-level anima-
> tion students. The professionals' feedback cascades into classrooms in
> every corner of the country and reaches places where students really
> need the mentoring and encouragement. It's about leveling the playing
> field. Sure, not everyone we reach will become a professional, but
> many go to college and most have a chance to engage in an expressive
> arts experience they might not have ever enjoyed. All of these kids will
> at least have the opportunity to give it a shot. (Sito 2008)

At the Met in Sacramento, students use Web 2.0 tools to collaborate
and create dynamic virtual learning spaces. Kimberley, whose mother is
going through cancer treatment in San Francisco, streams recorded audio
and screencasts of science lectures. She also submits assignments, takes
tests and quizzes, and chats with her science instructor, all while living at a
relative's home a hundred miles away. Without these tools, the family emergency would probably have put Kimberley far behind in her junior year.

Another Met Sacramento student, a high performing junior, rarely
sets foot in a traditional classroom. He spends his days working on a two-
year-long film project, attending college classes, and reviewing rubrics
and expectations for high school through shared Google documents and
interactive spaces in Schoology, the school's course management soft-
ware. He'll be able to complete his senior thesis project, autobiography,
and valedictory speech without taking any formal classes on campus.

# COME-BACK PROGRAMS

Leaving-to-learn options can also help learners who have dropped out and now want to return to school. (In many cases, students who drop out eventually crave and value learning much more than those who stay.) The typical high school has little or no capacity to accommodate them, although many school districts provide some form of GED (General Education Diploma) preparation. Many more opportunities are needed if schools are to engage these young people in productive learning. Schools need to create what Ralph Caplan (2008) has called "programs of resumed engagement."

As the late John Wooden, the most successful basketball coach in history, stated so eloquently, "The 'final score' is not the final score" (Wooden and Jamison 1997, 106). The final score on the basketball court or on a standardized test is not the final score, nor does it reflect the often-temporary circumstances of out-of-school youth. The final score is success over time. As the late Reverend Frederick Eikerenkoetter "Ike" Jr. observed, "When you discover who you are, it doesn't matter what you've been" (Richardson 2011).

The learning trajectory of one of our students proves the Reverend's observation. Andre grew up in a poor neighborhood of Philadelphia, read voraciously, attended a subpar public high school, and, after a few years languishing in classes, slid out of school. He turned his life around by enrolling in YouthBuild (a high school program for "overage and undercredited" young people) and starting a youth voice organization. Andre continued his reading and enrolled in a college course, paid for with stipends he earned through rigorous service to his community through AmeriCorps. He delivered keynote addresses and spoke on panels at a number of national conferences. Andre graduated from Hampshire College in 2012.

The GI Bill of Rights is an inspiration for what we call come-back programs. Some have argued that, along with the Civil Rights Act, the GI Bill was the most influential educational policy of the twentieth century.

It stimulated the advancement of adult education and community colleges in the United States, dramatically increasing college graduation rates. Some benefits provided by the Bill continue for today's returning war veterans.

Several of the GI Bill's features and components align with students' expectations regarding their education. The returning veterans had considerable experience and expected schools to recognize that experience when they developed courses and learning programs. They wanted more practical explanations and more hands-on work. They wanted labs that addressed research and practice. Because returning veterans had vouchers to pay for their education, colleges were eager to accommodate their needs and preferences (think "deeper four" mattering and fitting) and provided a cornucopia of programs and courses that did so. Sometimes veterans helped create and develop the programs.

We learn from the GI Bill and our own experience that it is difficult to attract dropouts back to learning unless the settings for that learning are very different from traditional schools and have the promise of success—a high school diploma, certification, a work and career pathway. The important features and components of a come-back program are not much different from those of Big Picture Learning schools:

- Personalized learning plans that are based on students' interests, needs, and choices and that include strong personal accountability and self-assessment.

- One-stop access to the support services essential for keeping participants focused on productive learning and work.

- Places for youth to obtain just-in-time learning: online learning, tutoring, classes, and certifications linked to work and services.

- Paid mentored internships in which participants learn both academic and technical skills and which lead to job-specific readiness certificates and productive work.

- Postsecondary options that include community colleges and technical schools.

Dropping out should never be an option, but pursuing great out-of-school learning opportunities should be, and schools should energetically support these choices and engagements as part of every student's learning trajectory. In this way, schools can fit the student to the school, the school to the student.

Implementing leaving-to-learn programs is a large, multiyear undertaking. Even without a fully developed program, however, schools, districts, and states can begin to reap benefits with carefully chosen first steps that address students' expectations.

Chapter

# 8

# SUPPORTING
# LEAVING TO LEARN

*If a child is to keep alive his inborn sense of wonder,*
*he [or she] needs the companionship of at least one*
*adult who can share it, rediscovering with him the joy,*
*excitement and mystery of the world we live in.*

—RACHEL CARSON, *THE SENSE OF WONDER*

Developing a leaving-to-learn program requires some careful planning and implementation if the potential of learning outside school is to be realized. Even the most promising out-of-school learning resources can be squandered by sending students out without important scaffolding.

## THE BASIC TOOLS

What does it take for a school to support leaving to learn? There are five components:

1. *Plans*: (a) a comprehensive student learning plan that addresses important academic, career, and personal competencies; (b) a detailed specification of tasks to be accomplished; and (c) a plan

for documenting and demonstrating learning. These plans must be regularly adjusted to reflect new learning opportunities and new learning standards. Many states *require* that schools create a personalized learning plan for each student.

2. *Protocols*: both schoolwide and student-specific "rules of the road" regarding student safety and privacy, logistics, transportation, communication, assessment, and accreditation. Protocols specify expectations for student behavior in the workplace as it pertains to their career and personal competencies.

3. *People*: experts, expert practitioners, and peers with and from whom students can learn. All adults with whom the students work need to be screened, typically through local law enforcement agencies. Schools also need to provide orientation programs for mentors and internship coaches.

4. *Places*: specific organizations and contexts in which out-of-school learning will take place. They include community organizations, businesses, colleges, museums, and online learning platforms. In our experience there are plenty of appropriate out-of-school places for students to do productive learning and plenty of adults willing and able to help them.

5. *Portfolios* for presenting/displaying student learning and accomplishments. Students must be able to provide proof—artifacts, certifications, logs, journals, web pages, and audio- and video-tapes (analog or digital) of performances—that they have achieved specific competencies. Teachers must be able to review and validate the learning and the products/outcomes. An increasing number of schools use student portfolios to document meeting the Common Core learning standards and judge the quality of student learning.

# BEYOND THE BASIC TOOLS

Schools need to establish cultures, structures, and processes that support leaving-to-learn programs and address students' expectations. Undoubtedly, schools will need to manage all five components via technology. Further, schools need to use their existing resources (typically a per-pupil allocation from the school district and funds raised from private sources) to pay for student transportation, travel, and after-school programs. Important ways to support effective learning-to-learn programs are discussed next.

## DEVELOP A MULTIYEAR IMPLEMENTATION PLAN

Given the scope and complexity of a leaving-to-learn program, schools need to implement it in stages, starting simply and slowly and then gradually expanding opportunities. We recommend giving priority to engaging *all* students in at least some opportunities at the earliest stages. It's also important to link the learning accomplished in such experiences to in-school learning and award academic and graduate credit for it.

## HELP TEACHERS GET READY

Teachers will need to take on new roles, roles that evolve as the program expands. They become brokers of their students' out-of-school resources, serving as part-time travel agents, tour guides, talent scouts, coaches, and trainers. These new roles require education, training, and support. Most of our Big Picture Learning schools employ specialists who identify leaving-to-learn opportunities and initiate contact and establish relationships with mentors and coaches.

An advisor/teacher at our Big Picture Learning school in Rotterdam, the Netherlands, found just the right leaving-to-learn opportunities for two students, one at an airport, another at a hotel. Both young women had powerful dreams of careers but very troubled school and life histories, and they needed considerable support during their first foray into the workplace. However, their internships gave them the jump start they needed, and their desire to learn intensified. It's hard to say who was more excited about the out-of-school learning opportunities, the students or their advisor.

## ORGANIZE LEAVING-TO-LEARN PEOPLE AND PLACES

Schools must be able to tap into a diverse network of experts, expert practitioners, and peers with and from whom students can learn. Abundant learning resources and opportunities exist outside school, but teachers must organize and use them effectively to advance productive learning. This requires not only establishing a give-and-take relationship with the community but also aggressively expanding that relationship. Most Big Picture Learning schools set up and continually add to their databases of people and places that support out-of-school learning.

## GET STUDENTS READY

Schools need to teach students to manage their learning plans and their portfolios, ensure students' safety and overall well-being, and provide a rich array of leaving-to-learn resources. Most students new to leaving-to-learn programs start slowly but adapt quickly to the demands of learning outside the traditional classroom. Typically, Big Picture Learning schools provide some form of summer "boot camp" for incoming ninth graders as an orientation to this new kind of learning.

## REDESIGN HOW THE SCHOOL IS ORGANIZED

Warren Bennis and Robert Thomas (2002) contend that one cannot send a changed individual back to an unchanged organization. There is no sense wasting professional development resources on helping teachers take on new roles if schools do not create the organizational structures and cultures in which teachers and students learn and work. Successfully launching leaving-to-learn programs requires that schools change some of their traditional methods of operation. Here is a starter set:

- Longer and more flexible learning periods.

- Longer school days and school years.

- Alternatives to the disciplines as the primary organizational structure.

- Individual and group projects within and across the disciplines.

- Varied roles for faculty members.

- Outside experts and expert practitioners working alongside teachers.

Providing productive learning that responds to students' expectations requires a tolerance—better yet, a passion—for continually examining alternatives to existing practice and questioning what might be considered adequate or good enough. This is similar to the quest for rigor and craftsmanship schools expect of their students.

## REDESIGN THE SCHOOL PROGRAM AND CURRICULUM

Big Picture Learning schools wrap an entire curriculum around each student's interests and career goals. Students generally spend two days a week learning outside school in a business, community organization, or institution of higher learning. Key components are:

- Personalized curriculum. A customized learning program and pathway—essentially, a career academy—for each student that addresses essential learning standards. Big Picture Learning schools are small, and advisors (teachers) typically work with a cohort of students for all four high school years.

- Learning that challenges students to apply their academic skills and understanding to real-world problems they identify as they learn and work in their area of interest—particularly the career they want—outside school. Project-based learning focused on students' interests provides a context and structure for integrating academic, workplace, and personal competencies into holistic learning.

- Opportunities for students to work with adults in the careers to which students aspire.

- Embedded/integrated academic disciplines (including the arts and design), with a heavy emphasis on literacy and numeracy skills. Students receive direct instruction via classes, small groups, one-on-one tutoring, and online programs, as needed.

- Comprehensive, performance-based assessments as well as traditional assessments. Each quarter students demonstrate their skills and understanding through exhibitions of their work and successful completion of individual and group projects, service learning, college classes, and community-based internships.

- Parental involvement, supported through quarterly discussions of student learning plans, reviews of student work, and attendance at student exhibitions.

- Support for and follow-up of students' postsecondary learning and transition to a career.

## EMPLOY NEW AND EMERGING TECHNOLOGIES

Highly effective leaving-to-learn programs depend on new technologies for communication, collaboration, and coordination for their success. Online programs for managing learning help teachers and students configure in- and out-of-school learning into comprehensive (and coherent) modules that document important competencies and lead not only to diplomas but also to certificates. Technology tools also help teachers and students manage the five components of leaving-to-learn support: plans, protocols, people, places, and portfolios.

## LEARNING COMMUNITIES

Schools need to help students develop social as well as intellectual capital. Affinity groups are an important part of highly personalized learning. Personalization requires that students participate not only in various in-school learning communities but also in out-of-school communities and social networks centered around their interests. Strong relationships with mentors and coaches in the world outside school help students build valuable social capital.

# CREATING ALTERNATIVE LEARNING ENVIRONMENTS

If, as Ralph Caplan has suggested, schools have a primary responsibility to create effective learning environments, they need to change the way they look inside even as they take advantage of the world outside. Although our Big Picture Learning schools have always looked different from traditional schools, we continue to look for places and spaces that inspire further change.

One source of inspiration is the Apple Store, now an icon in many large cities throughout the world. Since the first stores opened in 2001, we have spent numerous hours in many of these stores around the country, sometimes as customers but always as amateur anthropologists and ethnographers. (We wrote about this in an October 2009 *Kappan* article with Loran Newsom.) We find that what goes on in an Apple Store is a harbinger of how learning, working, and playing can be merged in a wide range of twenty-first-century venues, including schools.

Some may think that regarding a retail store as a learning place or community is odd and that learning how to use technological tools has no intellectual capital. However, there is ample reason to view the Apple Store—both as a physical space and as a link to a virtual space—as a prototypical learning environment, one in which an enterprising team of talented teachers could construct and implement a comprehensive and challenging learning program both in a physical location and on the Cloud.

The Apple Store is designed for selling, but it is also designed for learning. Apple's culture—its knowledge and values—embraces learning and learners. Nearly half the store is devoted to playing and learning. Indeed, the play area up front has a lot in common with a typical kindergarten classroom; the Studio, with a graduate seminar; and the Genius

Bar, with a lab or apprenticeship. In its artfully designed store space, Apple merges products with services for a unique experience in which customers see themselves as learners able to master valuable skills. By developing this type of agency, Apple has created a physical and virtual community in which people share a common story.

Experienced educators know that the learning environment—the physical, psychological, cultural, social, technological, and organizational elements—is as important as the learning opportunities themselves. Apple Store designers have followed this credo in creating a learning environment devoted to these elements. More than a school, museum, or library, the space and experience provide all who enter a chance to figure out what they need and, at the same time, browse and learn, both intentionally and serendipitously.

One question the Apple Store designers certainly addressed was how to design a store and an experience that gets people to come back again and again and buy again and again. In that spirit, we ask how might schools design a learner experience that motivates every student to engage in deep and sustained learning and choose to do that kind of learning for the rest of their lives?

What if, for example, schools deliberately designed learning opportunities and environments that were deeply engaging and motivating and actually helped young people learn powerfully within their many areas of interest? What if schools' most powerful learning spaces were not classrooms hung off long, bleak corridors but artists' studios, coffee shops, garages, makerspaces, and machine shops? What if these alternative learning places and spaces were increasingly more important than traditional school spaces in helping learners develop important skills and understanding?

Technology will be a critical enabler for connecting schools with out-of-school learning environments such as the Apple Store and for transforming in-school learning environments as well. Social and professional computer networks and "wiki" capacities can support learning. The many thousands of Internet how-to sites allow anyone to learn and practice how to do just about anything. What all these resources require is a framework, a system for helping each learner make sense of these resources and integrate them into a personalized learning plan. Technology will disrupt as well as enable, challenging and frustrating schools that merely want to automate their current designs in a quest for efficiency and effectiveness. Educators who listen to what new and emerging technologies are saying will hear the message of fundamental and highly disruptive change.

Learning environments such as the Apple Store are all around us, from theme-based cruise ships that focus on interests and hobbies to storefront creative writing centers and do-it-yourself fab labs. Big Picture Learning schools have found great learning environments in all manner of community and workplace settings (although doing so often requires creativity and ingenuity).

Schools also need to tap into out-of-school learning places that appeal to young people and engage them in productive learning. These are what Ray Oldenburg (1989) calls "third places" (the home and the workplace are the first and second), where people congregate and form multipurpose communities. Schools need to infuse learning opportunities into third places where their students congregate; give credit for learning wherever and whenever it occurs; and provide expert practitioners who join teachers in working with students. Schools need to come up with new ways of credentialing learning that are based on demonstrations of skills and understanding developed in any setting.

For young people who have given up on the traditional school system, a leaving-to-learn program can be a powerful magnet to bring them back and help them develop productive lives. But you may be thinking, *Leaving to learn is a great idea, but there is no way I can make those changes in my school,* and we understand. Leaving to learn is not for the faint of heart. Although leaving-to-learn programs can be implemented gradually over several years, the basic organizational structure must be in place to take even the first steps. If you are not ready to make those changes, it may be best to look for another approach to school reform. But you may have to relinquish any thoughts of delivering on students' expectations and resign yourself to living with high dropout rates and even higher levels of student disengagement.

## STUDENTS' EXPECTATIONS

# The New Imperatives

THE STORIES OF DROPOUTS—FAMOUS, NEAR FAMOUS, AND NOT YET
FAMOUS—HAVE INFORMED AND INSPIRED MUCH OF OUR WORK.
HOWEVER, OUR CONCERN FOR DROPOUTS, WHILE NOT MISPLACED, DOES
NOT ADDRESS THE BREADTH AND DEPTH OF THE PROBLEMS FACING
SCHOOLS. A DANGEROUSLY LARGE PERCENTAGE OF STUDENTS, WHILE
NOT AT "ESCAPE VELOCITY," ARE NEVERTHELESS DISENGAGED FROM
PRODUCTIVE LEARNING. OUR CHALLENGE, THEREFORE, IS NOT MERELY
TO REDUCE THE NUMBER OF DROPOUTS BUT TO MAKE SCHOOL A MORE
ENGAGING LEARNING PLACE FOR ALL STUDENTS.

LEAVING-TO-LEARN PROGRAMS CAN HELP SCHOOLS ADDRESS THAT
CHALLENGE, BUT IMPLEMENTING AND SUSTAINING SUCH PROGRAMS
WILL REQUIRE THAT SCHOOLS REDESIGN THEMSELVES. NEW SCHOOL
POLICIES, STRUCTURES, AND CULTURES ARE NEEDED TO SUPPORT NEW
PRACTICES. THE PREVIOUS CHAPTERS HAVE FOCUSED ON THE DETAILS
OF SUPPORTING THIS REDESIGN AND ITS IMPLEMENTATION.

AS WITH MOST SCHOOL REFORMS, HOWEVER, THIS WORK IS NOT
FOR THE SCHOOLS ALONE. IT WILL "TAKE A VILLAGE" TO SUPPORT
SCHOOLS AS THEY UNDERTAKE THE WORK. THE NEXT CHAPTER
DESCRIBES THE SUPPORT WE THINK IS NEEDED AND WHO NEEDS TO HELP
AND HOW. OUR FINAL CHAPTER LOOKS OUT A BIT—AT THE WORLD WE
ARE COMING TO, IF YOU WILL—AND SUGGESTS A FEW MACROLEVEL
CONSIDERATIONS FOR SCHOOL REFORM.

Chapter

9

# WHAT HAVE WE LEARNED?

*In Italy, for thirty years under the Borgias, they had warfare,
terror, murder, and bloodshed, but they produced Michelangelo,
Leonardo da Vinci, and the Renaissance. In Switzerland, they
had brotherly love, they had 500 years of democracy and peace,
and what did that produce? The cuckoo clock.*

—ORSON WELLES, AS HARRY LIME IN *THE THIRD MAN*

Recall the questions that guide this book:

- What do young people want from their schools?

- How can leaving-to-learn programs significantly increase the number of young people who stay deeply engaged in productive learning through high school graduation?

- What are the essential design features and components of leaving-to-learn and come-back programs?

- What changes will educators need to make in their schools to support leaving-to-learn and come-back programs?

Why students drop out (see figure on p. 120) has been well researched. Numerous reports cite variations of four big reasons: academic failure, behavioral problems, life events, and disinterest. But, as we have said, it's deeper than we think. Our experience in our own schools and in others reveals four deeper causes for disengagement and dropping out—fitting out, not in; mattering, or not; overlooked talents and interests; and

The Big Four

ACADEMIC FAILURE
BEHAVIOR
LIFE EVENTS
DISINTEREST

The Deeper Four

Not Mattering
Not Fitting In
Unrecognized Talents & Interests
Restrictions

restrictions. These "deeper four" not only provide more insight into the reasons for widespread disengagement but also suggest how schools might intervene to reduce the dropout rate and engage all students in productive learning.

Researchers have calculated the cost to society of dropouts but have missed the significantly larger cost of disengaged students who graduate from high school but are nonetheless unprepared for lifelong learning and whose talents and potential have been sadly ignored, often because those talents lie outside the traditional subject matter focus of a cognitive/abstract curriculum.

Using "the deeper four," we have articulated a series of students' expectations (see next figure) and maintain that the failure to address those expectations contributes significantly to the high levels of student disengagement from productive learning—the larger context in which the

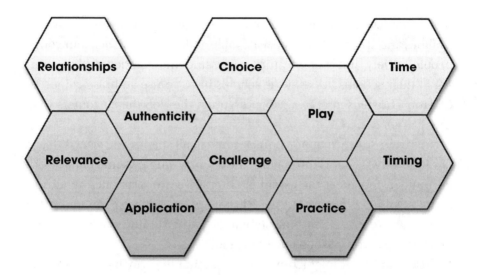

dropout problem exists. Schools can use students' expectations to guide their redesign of learning opportunities and learning environments.

While we applaud our country's efforts to identify a "common core" of learning standards, we are troubled by narrow definitions of what constitutes success and how to achieve and assess it. We prefer an "uncommon core" of standards and believe that what schools consider "high expectations" are actually quite low. Moreover, even if schools were to achieve those expectations, it would likely not be nearly enough to make a difference either for the students themselves or for society. The success now being sought—passing scores on reading, math, and science tests—is a mere table stake in the global economy, where high school and college graduates in many other countries achieve equally good test scores and work productively for a fraction of our costs in the United States.

Schools therefore need to address different and much higher expectations. They need to focus on graduating young people who have a positive perspective on learning and are prepared to continue learning for the rest of their lives. Such learning must focus on more than just competence in a narrow set of skills; it must address essential and up to now largely ignored competencies—creativity, innovation, and entrepreneurism, for starters—and aspire to the craftsmanship and mastery that advance all trades, services, and professions and to the artistry that advances our sensibilities and spirits. That is the real "value added" that will help our young people, society, and economy thrive. Few students experience such learning in their schools. It's as if the schools have, to use a phrase coined by Clayton Christensen et al. (2007), forgotten the "job the customers were trying to get done."

Leaving-to-learn opportunities come in all shapes and sizes. While a few innovative schools throughout the country employ some of these opportunities, few meet the essential criteria we propose: open to all students as an integral part of their learning plans, addressed to important academic and career learning standards, and awarding academic credit for learning accomplished outside school.

Developing, implementing, and maintaining leaving-to-learn programs make considerable demands of schools, requiring new and expanded roles for teachers and a much more fluid and flexible organizational structure and culture that are integrally connected with the world outside. This much openness to the world is important if schools are to maintain their currency as next-generation learning organizations.

You may not agree with all our perspectives on the problems or with all the solutions we have proposed, but on this you must agree—schools are facing a serious crisis that is much deeper and more pervasive than the dangerously high dropout rate. The high levels of student disengagement threaten to weaken our schools further at a time when we need them to create the next generation of citizens and workers who will lead our country in this century.

Leaving to learn is neither snake oil nor a magic cure-all. To embrace it fully is to significantly expand learning opportunities for all young people—to keep in school the students who are leaning toward leaving and bring back those who have made the leap, physically or psychologically. The objective is this: significantly increase the level of student engagement in productive learning and, as a by-product, reap a much reduced dropout rate. Leaving-to-learn programs as we have defined them provide new and exciting learning opportunities and learning environments for young people in our secondary schools and a bold new strategy for redesigning schools. Recall Gary Hamel's observation from the preface, "strategy *is* revolution; everything else is just tactics" (1996). Tactical changes—think deck chairs on the *Titanic*—will not deliver the results we need.

# So What?

What do the school system and the larger social and economic systems within which it operates need to do to support leaving-to-learn programs? For starters, we suggest embracing important principles, policies, and practices.

## Principles

Schools will:

- Develop the whole person—not just a competent worker but also a lifelong learner, family leader, and engaged citizen, healthy in mind, heart, and body.

- Provide students with a voice and a choice regarding their education.

- Help students discover and develop their interests and talents.

- Offer students numerous ways to show what they know and can do.

- Engage parents and families in their children's education and in the school community.

- Reach out to their communities, aggressively seeking opportunities for service and establishing relationships for advancing student learning and development.

- Form strong and lasting partnerships with industry and postsecondary institutions.

- Remain dynamic and open to ongoing change, responding nimbly and quickly to what is happening in the workplace, in society, and particularly in the lives of students.

## POLICIES

Based on these principles, schools must:

- Employ a broad and multidimensional definition of success and address a much broader range of competencies across all the disciplines to achieve different—and better—results.

- Focus on competency, shifting from assessing time spent in a classroom to assessing real-world performances and contexts that demonstrate skill, understanding, and dispositions.

- Provide personalized programs of study for all students, customized to address their interests and talents.

- Create a secondary school system that helps each student pursue his or her learning plan regardless of the career path he or she has chosen.

- Allow expert practitioners into schools to work alongside teachers.

- Use retirees with interests that match the students', merging seniors' wisdom and knowledge of craft with students' energy and enthusiasm.

- Get teachers out of schools by expanding their roles to include leading and facilitating experts and expert practitioners in helping students learn within their areas of interest.

- Aggressively promote out-of-school learning by developing individual student learning plans that incorporate leaving-to-learn opportunities for all students.

- Broaden assessments beyond the basic skills to include essential academic, career, and personal competencies.

- Provide academic credit for competencies developed outside school.

- Help dropouts to return to school by reaching out to young people without a high school diploma and giving them the opportunity to create a formal learning program centered around their interests or the work they do.

Few of these principles and policies are reflected in current national priorities, which, you may have noticed, also become the priorities of states and municipalities. Yet most of the failures of prevailing school designs can be traced to a violation of one or more of these principles. Moreover, the problem is not merely a few poor policies; it's a worldview of schools that is at odds with what research and insightful experience tell us about learners and learning.

This lack of national and state leadership is not for want of thoughtful policy recommendations. For example, a recent report, *Learn Anytime, Anywhere: Rethinking How Students Earn Credit Beyond School Hours* (2012), issued by The After-School Corporation (TASC), in New York City, makes an insightful plea for awarding academic credit for real-world learning.

## PRACTICES

In addition to adopting these and similar policies, school districts need to examine existing practices that impede the full implementation of leaving-to-learn programs. We have cited several throughout this book: Carnegie units as a means of accrediting learning, a rigid curriculum scope and sequence, subject-based organizational structures, restrictive schedules, and no recognition of learning accomplished outside school. The most serious impediment is the failure to embrace the community as a place of learning where young people form relationships with adult mentors with similar interests, build their social capital, and add value.

We recall in the early days of our first school, The Met, in Providence, Rhode Island, when our practice of having all our students learn outside school two days each week raised concerns. Wishing to make the point that school need not be so fixed a place, Dennis Littky, co-principal, found a small block of wood, printed *The Met* on it, and told skeptics that by taking the block with them when they went out to work and learn in out-of-school settings students would still be "at school." The joke helped make the point that school can be anywhere productive learning is taking place.

Schools need to retool the way they watch for signs of disengagement. For example, perhaps students' expectations could be used as the basis for regularly administered surveys of students and their parents to assess how well schools are meeting those expectations. Schools might use an Apgar-type assessment (a score devised by the anesthesiologist,

Dr. Virginia Apgar, in 1952 to assess the health of a newborn) to obtain real-time data on how well they are meeting students' expectations. Schools might even replace their early warning system for potential dropouts with one assessing potential and actual disengagement.

Schools must redefine and reconstitute the teacher's role. Many teachers would welcome these new roles and responsibilities but will undoubtedly point out that they would be frustrated unless schools put in place organizational structures and cultures for maximizing their talents and energy. In short, schools need to meet their teachers' as well as their students' expectations!

All of this is messy work. Schools and teachers also use the learning funnel we describe in Chapter 6 to grapple with the mysteries of learning and learners and schools and schooling. Indeed, this book might be seen as a heuristic of sorts, a strategy for working things out, for creating—and continually recreating—the algorithms and codes that govern schools, many of which are not working. This important state and school district work is being neglected in the madness of low-level instruction and testing that plague our schools, particularly big city schools serving poor and minority youth. The so-called out-of-the-box thinking driving the current design for schools and learning is exhausted. Our country needs to create new boxes to think outside of.

# WHO CAN HELP?

Although the schools must shoulder much of the load for developing and maintaining leaving-to-learn programs, many others in the "village" can help. As schools embrace the community, including virtual communities, the number of helpers will increase.

## POLITICAL LEADERS AND POLICY MAKERS

Those who set educational policy need to embrace the principles and policies we have identified and retire existing policies and regulations that impede the development of schools as dynamic, nimble institutions that respond to students' expectations and provide productive learning for all students.

## PARENTS

Parents are their children's first talent spotters, coaches, travel agents, and mentors. Schools can help parents enhance these roles. Parents can investigate how their schools are addressing students' expectations and monitor the relationship their children have with their schools. They can discuss their children's interests and talents with teachers and contribute to the development of their learning plans. Parents can partner with teachers to watch for signs of disengagement and together formulate interventions.

## EMPLOYERS

Employers can support leaving-to-learn programs by providing the learning environments and experts that students want to connect with in pursuing their career interests. Employers are a rich source of mentors and coaches who, in concert with classroom teachers, can blend in-school and out-of-school learning.

The workplace is a multifaceted setting: a studio, a manufacturing plant, a hospital emergency room, an airport, a farm, a social service agency. Schools need to work with employers to get young people into such workplaces early and often. Educators and employers can exploit the power of social networking and authentically situated learning. This is what comes naturally to young people. They want to learn from people who have the skills they need for the work they want to do. They want to be these people in the future, to dream, tinker, discover, and invent new ways of working to benefit yet another generation. These young people are, as author Neil Postman (1982) once observed, "the living messages we send to a time we will not see."

Chapter

# 10

# WHAT IN THE WORLD
# ARE WE COMING TO?

*Always go too far, because that's where you will find the truth.*

—ALBERT CAMUS

Leaving-to-learn programs, however well designed and implemented, are only one component of a school reform strategy. A school district contemplating truly systemic reform needs to employ numerous interventions to provide the learning opportunities and environments that productive learning and learners require. Here are our recommendations.

## ACT ON "THE DEEPER FOUR" BY ADDRESSING STUDENTS' EXPECTATIONS

If, as we have argued, four deeper factors lead many young people to drop out of high school and many more to disengage from learning, schools must establish new kinds of early warning systems focused on those factors. Schools must use students' expectations to guide their redesign of learning opportunities and learning environments. Young people need to feel that who they are matters to their teachers and that schools are trying to fit themselves to students even as they are asking students to fit into the school. Students want help from schools in discovering, developing, and using their talents.

## FOCUS ON PRODUCTIVE LEARNING

Think back to how Seymour Sarason (2004) influenced our definition of productive learning, underscoring the importance of its generative function, its power to engage students. Without that function, schools could be satisfied with mere competence at a time when craftsmanship, mastery, and artistry are so desperately needed. In Big Picture Learning schools, we refuse to stop at competence, because we know how much talent and potential our young people possess. We are determined to find and develop that talent and that potential. Unless schools and school districts adopt productive learning as their prime directive, no amount of reform is likely to make much difference.

## ADOPT NEW IMPERATIVES

Schools must adopt students' expectations as their new design requirements, their new "rules of engagement," and the new value they offer their students and their families. Umair Hague, in his recent book, *Betterness* (2011), suggests that traditional approaches to crafting strategy and developing tactics may no longer be useful. Instead, Hague advises, we need to think about bold, new initiatives based on design principles he calls "imperatives." Using Apple as an example, Hague notes that the company's strategy is less about market share and profitability (for educators, the counterpart is test scores), however important those may be, and more about the experience its customers will have with its products and services. Hague's insight is similar to Ralph Caplan's (2005) observation

> SCHOOLS MUST ADOPT STUDENTS' EXPECTATIONS AS THEIR NEW DESIGN REQUIREMENTS, THEIR NEW "RULES OF ENGAGEMENT," AND THE NEW VALUE THEY OFFER THEIR STUDENTS AND THEIR FAMILIES.

that the schools are responsible for providing the right environments for learning.

We agree and propose that these environments must be designed according to students' expectations or, better yet, schools' imperatives. Schools that adopt these imperatives will thrive as sources of productive learning for their students. Delivering on these imperatives will become a new form of schools' accountability to their students and society. Significantly increased student engagement will follow, as will a significantly reduced dropout rate. And students will experience the kind of success we have described.

## STUDENTS' EXPECTATIONS RESTATED AS IMPERATIVES FOR SCHOOLS

- We will know our students' interests, talents, and aspirations.
- We will start with, and wrap a program of study around, each student's interests, talents, aspirations, and needs.
- We will engage students in meaningful and valuable learning and work, in and out of school.
- We will give students opportunities to apply their learning in real-world settings and contexts.
- We will offer students choices in how their learning is designed and how their performances are assessed.
- We will challenge students to achieve levels of craftsmanship, mastery, and artistry in their performances.
- We will give students opportunities to experiment and discover within their areas of interest.
- We will give students opportunities for deep and sustained practice.
- We will provide customized learning schedules.
- We will give students opportunities to sequence their learning activities.

# CONDUCT RESEARCH AND DEVELOPMENT

Earlier we lamented the lack of solid research on true alternatives to traditional practice. Research addressing the following questions related to out-of-school learning will provide valuable answers for practitioners and policy makers alike:

- What does out-of-school learning look like in practice?

- How are traditional academics addressed in out-of-school learning?

- What are the facilitators of and impediments to implementing high-quality leaving-to-learn programs?

- What do students and teachers say about such programs?

- What impact do out-of-school learning experiences have on student learning?

- What competencies does out-of-school learning develop particularly well? For example, do students who do a lot of their learning outside school develop more competence in acquiring and using social capital?

- Do employers rate new hires with leaving-to-learn experiences as better prepared to learn in the workplace?

- Do students who participate in out-of-school learning programs do better in postsecondary learning?

# TAKE ON NEW CHALLENGES

Alternative learning organizations that appeal to young people will deliver on the imperatives creatively and often disruptively. Many of these alternatives will be enabled by technology. Some will be embedded in schools; others will flourish outside the traditional system. Challenges will proliferate.

As an example, take the offer that entrepreneur Peter Thiel (cofounder and ex-CEO of PayPal) made to under-twenty-year-olds through the Thiel Fellowship: Create a promising product or service and a compelling business model, and I will fund your start-up. What kind of learning does such an offer provoke? What does the résumé and portfolio of an applicant need to look like? While such a "learning opportunity" sits on the periphery of a high school or college curriculum, how and when does it enter the mainstream in true Clayton Christensen (*The Innovator's Dilemma*, 1997) mode?

Throughout this book we have, often and deliberately, referred to how great teachers meet their students' expectations. We know, firsthand, many outstanding teachers and principals. Many of them work in our schools, delivering on students' expectations every day. Recent surveys indicate that teacher morale in this country is at a new low. Could it be that schools are failing to deliver on the expectations teachers and principals have of their schools? That schools are failing to provide their faculties with great learning environments?

We are, as sociologist and psychologist Sherry Turkle (2005) has observed, in a "liminal moment" between the old and the new. Like Linus when his blanket is in the dryer or a molting lobster without the old hard shell, we are a bit unsure and therefore tentative and timid just when a bit of smart risk taking is in order. Certainly, on behalf of our young people, we should be ready to take those risks. Film director, screenwriter, and actress Elaine May once observed, "The only safe thing is to take a chance," or, as the French might say, "*Bon chance*" (Lahr 2005).

Schools need to take a chance on more than incremental improvements. They need, as a recent Ford automobile advertisement proclaimed, "bold moves." Yet, current conditions—political, educational, and economic—are not conducive to such moves. Instead, we see mostly timid approaches to innovation. The system focuses principals' and teachers' creativity and talents on raising test scores and complying with regulations rather than on providing productive learning. Schools are wasting the talents of their professionals as well as their students.

Janet Malcolm, writer and journalist on the staff of *The New Yorker*, has observed, "Creative work in any established system of thought takes place at the boundaries of the system, where its powers of explanation are least developed and its vulnerability to outside attack is most marked" (1997). At a time when our nation laments the decline in creativity and invention, it seems ever more imperative that schools create some significant alternatives to themselves, to think outside the box, the school box, that is. Such alternatives might question the need for all students to pass algebra or to attend a four-year college after high school graduation. Such alternatives might employ a wholly different structure for the school day focused not on subject areas but on the types of student work: projects, workshops, lectures, tinkering, exhibitions, and so forth. Teachers and principals must lead that redesign work.

# ESTABLISH NEW RELATIONSHIPS

As a society, we cannot expect to improve the relationships all of us have with our places of work and with our families and communities without repairing the relationship that students have with their schools. Schools must be "net zero" with respect to our planet's most valuable resource: our young people. No wasted talent! Let's go green on talent, aggressively seeking it out and developing it. It's hard to tell young people to live up to their potential when their schools are not living up to theirs.

AS A SOCIETY, WE CANNOT . . . IMPROVE [OUR] RELATIONSHIPS . . . WITH OUR PLACES OF WORK, . . . OUR FAMILIES AND COMMUNITIES WITHOUT REPAIRING THE RELATIONSHIP THAT STUDENTS HAVE WITH THEIR SCHOOLS.

Just as we call for a new relationship between young people and their schools based on the imperatives and productive learning, we call for a new set of relationships between schools and the larger community, itself an environment full of learning opportunities and resources. The "village" can provide the places where students can find the challenges and support they need to be the successful artists, craftspeople, family leaders, tradespeople, scientists, and citizens they wish to become. Schools must provide the policies and systems that allow students to get credit for their learning in and outside school walls.

# FIND NEW WAYS OF INNOVATING

Schools need to create and support a faculty that is skilled in and committed to relentless innovation—edgy as well as sustaining—in the interest of their students' learning. A culture and organizational structure for innovating requires a tolerance—make that a *passion*—for continually examining alternatives to existing practice. We call schools with such a culture Velcro organizations, because they so easily attract, embrace, and evaluate innovations for teaching and learning.

In their creation, charter schools were envisioned as Velcro organizations, but most of them are, at best, better versions of the failing public schools for which they were meant to be models. The absence of significant and widespread variation in what is taught and how it is assessed is a troubling signal. Velcro has become duct tape. Perhaps we need to revisit the original intentions and design charter schools around the imperatives.

Our own experience tells us that significant alternatives to the traditional system will be out of compliance with the narrow definitions of student success and with the regulations and protocols for how those outcomes must be achieved. We have observed with sadness many highly talented teachers and principals who struggle to innovate within such circumstances and are reminded of the local shop owner who complained, "If I'm in compliance, I'm out of business." Compliance with outdated policies and regulations puts schools out of the innovation business.

Improvements in the learning of all students, especially those from low-income families, will have to come as much from outside as inside schools. School leaders need to widen their vision of school reform to include efforts to rejuvenate learning for all and contribute to the economic and cultural development of the community.

Despite the failures of the current schooling system and the availa - bility of significantly different alternatives, we are not surprised by the unwillingness of educators—and noneducators as well—to accept these alternatives. Our explanation for this resistance is based on what the medical profession calls "the tomato effect" (Segen's Medical Dictionary

2012),[1] a label derived from the history of the tomato in North America. Although the tomato was a staple of the European diet as early as the mid-1500s, when it was first brought to the American colonies, it was regarded as poisonous, until the 1800s. That people in Europe were eating tomatoes without a problem for so long was not enough to change the minds of Europeans living in North America (Goodwin and Goodwin 1984). The history of medicine in this country is replete with examples of practices that were rejected out of hand because they did not conform to prevailing belief systems. We refuse to see what we do not believe and, conversely, see only what we do believe.

An even more pernicious phenomenon is what Dr. Frank Wilson (2012) calls the "rotten tomato effect," the continued use of a medicine that produces its intended effects but with serious side effects. At least in medicine, the side effects are measured; side effects in education are seldom mentioned, much less examined.

The current system of schooling privileges a paradigm that does not serve our young people or our society well. In maintaining the status quo, we run the risk of losing this and future generations of talent. By embracing the imperatives, we can offer educational opportunities to a diverse vanguard of students who possess exponential potential. It is worth the work.

Each year, hundreds of educators, policy makers, and foundation staff visit our highly successful Big Picture Learning schools and marvel at the work the students do. They extol the virtues of the school design—the organizational structure and culture—that support learning. Most leave, however, seemingly unwilling or unable to create in their own schools the very different organizational structure and culture required to realize those accomplishments. Instead, they settle for developing better versions of what they already have and are disappointed when they do not obtain significantly different results. Most policy makers and foundation staff

---

1. The "tomato effect" refers to rejection of an effective treatment for a disease for illogical reasons. This may occur when conventional logic dictates that a drug should have no therapeutic value or is toxic, as once occurred with aspirin.

leave bemoaning the challenges of "scaling" either the Big Picture Learning school design or the leaving-to-learn program. They fail to appreciate how artisanal are the changes required and how many assumptions and belief systems need to be deliberately challenged and then changed.

We like the distinction Charles Leadbeater (Ted.com 2010) makes between scaling as formulaic replication (think McDonald's) and proliferation (think Chinese restaurants). At Big Picture Learning, therefore, our goal is not to create replicas of our original school but to spread our design principles and help each school enhance its capacity to create a high-quality customized design based on Big Picture Learning's core features and components. Using our school imperatives as design requirements fits well with this notion of spread as the pathway to change. Our intent is that the imperatives "go viral" in this more artisanal and organic way.

Mark Twain was irreverent and irritating as much as he was entertaining. His humor softened the blows he rained on society and its institutions. We see ourselves as a bit irreverent and irritating to some—no one left unoffended, including ourselves, if you will. But, like Twain, we are eternal optimists, so we have an outsized optimism regarding the potential of schools to make a difference in the lives of their students.

Back in 1986, Steve Jobs bought 70 percent of Pixar from Lucasfilm's computer division with $5 million of his own money. At that time, Pixar was struggling mightily, and there seemed to be no market for its products. Jobs then invested another $5 million in the work of the company. Over the next nine years, Pixar had *not one* profitable quarter, yet Jobs continued to invest an additional $40 million and his own energy to keep the company going. He never gave up on Pixar, and ultimately his vision paid off, with *Toy Story* in 1995 (which featured our buddy, Mr. Potato Head!), and with the many other blockbusters that followed. In 2006, Jobs sold Pixar to Disney for approximately $7.4 billion (Isaacson 2011).

Jobs was famous (infamous?) for his unrelenting drive for the best design and the highest-quality products in the technology marketplace. His drive was fueled in part by the deep impatience that many highly successful people have with poor performance and poor quality. The Pixar story, however, reveals another facet of Jobs' personality. He had the patience and vision to wait nine years for Pixar's success. Jobs understood the potential of animation and kept his focus on that future as he waited for the world to recognize the rightness of his judgment.

We try to stay alert to the world our students will inherit and to think deeply and creatively about what it will take for them to be highly successful in that world. We continue to refine and expand our Big Picture Learning schools and work with others who wish to adopt some of our design's core features and components. The growing number of networks devoted to redesigning schools is encouraging. We play an active role in these networks to spread our school design principles, our imperatives, and our leaving-to-learn design. Our experience in these networks and with the growing number of schools working in "innovation zones" convinces us that schools can make the changes we have described.

In the world we are coming to—we should probably say the world already here—young people will increasingly look beyond traditional schools for their learning opportunities. We are convinced that by delivering a new kind of student experience based on the imperatives, schools can survive and, indeed, thrive. We are equally convinced that schools must provide, as a significant part of that experience, a leaving-to-learn program that embraces the world of learning outside schools and helps young people engage that world successfully. *It's imperative!*

# PREFACE

Adler, Bill. 1986. *The Cosby Wit: His Life and Humor*. New York: Carroll & Graf.

Als, Hilton. 1999. "A Pryor Love." *The New Yorker* (September 13).
    Available at www.newyorker.com/archive/1999/09/13/
    1999_09_13_068_TNY_LIBRY_000019041?currentPage=all.

Ayres, Alex. 1987. *The Wit and Wisdom of Mark Twain*. New York: Penguin.

Carlin, George, and Tony Hendra. 2009. *Last Words*. New York: Free Press.

Coster, Helen. 2010. "Millionaire High School Dropouts." *Forbes* magazine (January
    30). Available at www.forbes.com/2010/01/30/millionaires-without-high-
    school-diplomas-entrepreneurs-finance-millionaire.html.

Drell, Lauren. 2011. "We Don't Need No Education: Meet the Millionaire Dropouts."
    *Huffington Post*, February 9. Available at www.huffingtonpost.com/2011/02/09/
    we-dont-need-no-education-millionaire-dropouts_n_916319.html.

Gates Notes, The. 2010. *The Curious Classroom: Questions from Students Around the
    World*. The Gates Notes, LLC, January 21. Available at www.thegatesnotes.com/
    Curious-Classroom/SpecialFeature.aspx. Accessed February 1, 2010.

Gelly, Dave. 2002. *Stan Getz: Nobody Else but Me*. San Francisco: Backbeat Books.

Hamel, Gary. 1996. "Strategy as Revolution." *Harvard Business Review* 74 (4): 69–82.

John F. Kennedy Center for the Performing Arts, The. 2012. *The Kennedy Center Mark
    Twain Prize for Humor: Past Winners* 2012. Available at www.kennedy-
    center.org/programs/specialevents/marktwain/#history.

Marc Ecko Enterprises. 2008. *Marc Ecko Enterprises: About Marc*. Available at
    www.marcecko.com/#/About-Marc/?query=7ce5bad0b9da56f160c011aea18409b7.

Maxwell, John C. 2010. "The Dropout with a Doctorate." *Business Inquirer*, October 16.
    Available at http://business.inquirer.net/money/columns/view/20101016-
    298085/The-dropout-with-a-doctorate.

*New York Times*. 1907. "Great Pageant at Oxford: Mark Twain Delighted—
    Three Thousand Performers Engaged." *New York Times*, June 28.
    Available at http://query.nytimes.com/gst/abstract.html
    ?res=F40611F8385A15738DDDA10A94DE405B878CF1D3.
    Accessed May 31, 2012.

Paine, Albert Bigelow. 1916. *The Boys' Life of Mark Twain: The Story of a Man Who
    Made the World Laugh and Love Him*. New York: Harper & Brothers.

Public Broadcasting Service (PBS). 2009. *The Eleventh Annual Kennedy Center Mark Twain Prize Celebrating George Carlin* (2008). Available at www.pbs.org/weta/twain2008/.

Public Broadcasting Service (PBS) Video. 2009. *The Twelfth Annual Kennedy Center Mark Twain Prize Honors Bill Cosby* (2009). Available at http://video.pbs.org/video/1317746583#.

Ramachandran, Vilayanur S. 2004. "Phantoms in the Brain" [Lecture 1]. *Reith Lectures 2003: The Emerging Mind*. BBC. Available at www.bbc.co.uk/radio4/reith2003/lecture1.shtml. Accessed November 10, 2011.

Smith, Ronald L. 1997. *Cosby: The Life of a Comedy Legend*. New York: Prometheus Books.

*Time* magazine. 1977. "Lily . . . Ernestine . . . Tess . . . Lupe . . . Edith Ann. . . ." Available at www.time.com/time/magazine/article/0,9171,914863,00.html.

# INTRODUCTION

Balfanz, Robert, John M. Bridgeland, Mary Bruce, and Joanna Hornig Fox. 2012. *Building a Grad Nation: Progress and Challenge in Ending the High School Dropout Epidemic* [annual update]. Washington, DC: Alliance for Excellent Education, America's Promise Alliance, Civic Enterprises, and Everyone Graduates Center at Johns Hopkins University.

Biggs, Barton. 2006. *Hedgehogging*. Hoboken, NJ: John Wiley & Sons.

Gewertz, Catherine. 2011. "Higher Education Is Goal of GED Overhaul." *Education Week*, November 14: 1, 16–17.

Obama, Barack. 2009. *Remarks of President Barack Obama—as Prepared for Delivery, Address to Joint Session of Congress, Tuesday, February 24*. Available at www.whitehouse.gov/the_press_office/Remarks-of-President-Barack-Obama-Address-to-Joint-Session-of-Congress/.

Powell, Alma. 2008. "The Dropout Epidemic in the U.S. and Cross-Sector Solutions." Keynote address presented to America's Promise Alliance, April 30, Washington, DC: America's Promise Alliance.

Princiotta, Daniel, and Ryan Reyna. 2009. *Achieving Graduation for All: A Governor's Guide to Dropout Prevention and Recovery*. Washington, DC: National Governors Association Center for Best Practices. Available at www.nga.org/files/live/sites/NGA/files/pdf/0910ACHIEVINGGRADUATION.pdf.

Robinson, Ken. 2001. *Out of Our Minds: Learning to Be Creative*. West Sussex, UK: Capstone.

Sarason, Seymour. 2004. *And What Do YOU Mean by Learning?* Portsmouth, NH: Heinemann.

White House, The, and President Barack Obama. 2012. *2012 State of the Union Address*, January 25. Available at www.whitehouse.gov/photos-and-video/video/2012/01/25/2012-state-union-address-enhanced-version#transcript. Accessed April 5, 2012.

## CHAPTER 1

Auden, W. H. [1938] n.d. "Musée des Beaux Arts." Retrieved from http://english.emory.edu/classes/paintings&poems/auden.html.

Bailey, Thomas, and Vanessa Smith Morest. 1998. "Preparing Youth for Employment." In *The Forgotten Half: American Youth and Young Families, 1998–2008*, edited by Samuel Halperin. Washington, DC: American Youth and Policy Forum.

Balfanz, Robert, John M. Bridgeland, Mary Bruce, and Joanna Hornig Fox. 2012. *Building a Grad Nation: Progress and Challenge in Ending the High School Dropout Epidemic* (annual update). Washington, DC: Alliance for Excellent Education, America's Promise Alliance, Civic Enterprises, and Everyone Graduates Center at Johns Hopkins University.

Balfanz, Robert, John M. Bridgeland, Joanna Hornig Fox, and Laura A. Moore. 2011. *Building a Grad Nation: Progress and Challenge in Ending the High School Dropout Epidemic* (2010–2011 annual update). Washington, DC: America's Promise Alliance.

Batty, David. 2010. "Jessica Watson, the Girl Who Sailed Round the World, Comes Home to Cheers." *The Guardian*, May 15. Available at www.guardian.co.uk/world/2010/may/15/jessica-watson-sailed-world-home.

Big Picture Learning. 2004. In-house letter.

Bloom, Benjamin S. 1985. "The Nature of the Study and Why It Was Done." In *Developing Talent in Young People*, edited by Benjamin S. Bloom. New York: Ballantine.

Bridgeland, John M., John J. Dilulio, and Karen Burke Morison. 2006. *The Silent Epidemic: Perspectives of High School Dropouts*. Washington, DC: Civic Enterprises and Peter D. Hart Research Associates for the Bill & Melinda Gates Foundation.

British Broadcasting Company (BBC) News US & Canada. 2011. "U.S. Teenager Jordan Romero Sets Seven-Peak Record," December 25. Available at www.bbc.co.uk/news/world-us-canada-16328714.

Brown, Brené. 2010. *The Gifts of Imperfection: Let Go of Who You Think You're Supposed to Be and Embrace Who You Are*. Center City, MN: Hazelden.

Cameron, James. 2012. Personal communication.

Cole, Tom. 2010. "Django Reinhardt: 100 Years of Hot Jazz." *National Public Radio*, January 23. Available at www.npr.org/templates/story/story.php?storyId=122865782.

Csikszentmihalyi, Mihaly, and Barbara Schneider. 2000. *Becoming Adult: How Teenagers Prepare for the World of Work*. New York: Basic Books.

Darnton, Kate, Kayce Freed Jennings, and Lynn Sherr, eds. 2007. *Peter Jennings: A Reporter's Life*. Philadelphia: Perseus Books.

DuTemple, Lesley A. 2000. *Jacques Cousteau*. Minneapolis: Lerner.

Epstein, Robert. 2007. "The Myth of the Teen Brain." *Scientific American Mind* April/May: 56–63.

Gelfand, Tatiana V., and Tatiana I. Gelfand. 2009. Israel Moiseevich Gelfand website. Under *Work in Education*. Available at www.israelmgelfand.com/edu_work.html. Accessed April 9, 2012.

Goleman, Daniel. 1986. "Rethinking the Value of Intelligence Tests." *New York Times*, November 9. Available at www.nytimes.com/1986/11/09/education/rethinking-the-value-of-intelligence-tests.html?pagewanted=all.

Hollander, Jason. 2007. "A Cinematic Master Reveals the Spirit That Drives Him to Follow Roads Not Taken." *NYU Alumni Magazine* Fall (9). Available at www.nyu.edu/alumni.magazine/issue09/feature_ang.html.

Hughes, Langston. [1940] 1993. *The Big Sea: An Autobiography*. New York: Macmillan: Hill & Wang.

Mencken, H. L. 1928. "Travail." *Baltimore Evening Sun*, Oct. 8. Reprinted in *A Mencken Chrestomathy* (1982; New York: Vintage Books).

Nietzsche, Friedrich. 2007. *Ecce Homo: How One Becomes What One Is*. Translated by Duncan Large. Oxford, UK: Oxford University Press.

Noguera, Pedro A. 2004. "Transforming High Schools." *Educational Leadership* 61 (8): 26–31. Available at www.ascd.org/publications/educational-leadership/may04/vol61/num08/-Transforming-High-Schools.aspx.

Paul, Les. 2007. *Les Paul—Chasing Sound!* [DVD]. In *American Masters*. Available at www.youtube.com/watch?v=5yz9lmLlSsc.

Pink, Daniel H. 2009. *Drive: The Surprising Truth About What Motivates Us*. New York: Riverhead Books.

Robison, John Elder. 2011a. *Be Different: Adventures of a Free-Range Aspergian with Practical Advice for Aspergians, Misfits, Families, and Teachers*. New York: Random House.

———. 2011b. *About John*. Blog. Available at http://johnrobison.com/about-john.php. Accessed January 3, 2012.

Sacks, Oliver. 1999. "Brilliant Light." *The New Yorker*, December 20, 56–73.

Shimura, Tomoya. 2010. "Romero Welcomed Home After Climbing Mount Everest." *Victorville* (Calif.) *Daily Press*, June 10. Available at www.vvdailypress.com/articles/lake-19794-bear-mount.html.

Sosniak, Lauren A. 1989. "From Tyro to Virtuoso: A Long-Term Commitment to Learning." In *Music and Child Development: Proceedings of the 1987 Biology of Music Making Conference*, edited by Frank R. Wilson and Franz L. Roehmann, 274–90. St. Louis: MMB Music.

Willms, J. Douglas, Sharon Friesen, and Penny Milton. 2009. *What Did You Do in School Today? Transforming Classrooms Through Social, Academic and Intellectual Engagement*. Toronto, ON: Canadian Education Association.

Wilson, Frank R. 1998. *The Hand: How Its Use Shapes the Brain, Language, and Human Culture*. New York: Pantheon.

# CHAPTER 2

Anderson, Jenny. 2011. "From Finland, an Intriguing School-Reform Model." *New York Times*, December 12. Available at http://www.nytimes.com/2011/12/13/education/from-finland-an-intriguing-school-reform-model.html?pagewanted=all.

Arnold, Karen. 1995. *Lives of Promise: What Becomes of High School Valedictorians*. San Francisco: Jossey-Bass.

Bronowski, Jacob. 1976. *The Ascent of Man*. Boston: Little, Brown.

Conant, James Bryant. 1940. "Education for a Classless Society: The Jeffersonian Tradition." *The Atlantic Monthly* (May). Available at www.theatlantic.com/past/docs/issues/95sep/ets/edcla.htm.

Coyle, Daniel. 2009. *The Talent Code: Greatness Isn't Born. It's Grown. Here's How*. New York: Bantam.

Csikszentmihalyi, Mihaly. 1996. *Creativity: Flow and the Psychology of Discovery and Invention*. New York: HarperCollins.

Encyclopaedia Britannica. 2012. *Uno Cygnaeus*. Available at www.britannica.com/EBchecked/topic/148261/Uno-Cygnaeus. Accessed March 13, 2012.

Gladwell, Malcolm. 2008. *Outliers: The Story of Success*. New York: Little, Brown.

Hancock, LynNell. 2011. "Why Are Finland's Schools Successful?" *Smithsonian* magazine (September). Available at www.smithsonianmag.com/people-places/Why-Are-Finlands-Schools-Successful.html.

Handy, Charles. 1990. *The Age of Unreason*. Boston: Harvard Business School.

Kaplan, Ann. 1998. *Maslow on Management*. New York: John Wiley & Sons.

Kirn, Walter. 2005. "Lost in the Meritocracy: How I Traded an Education for a Ticket to the Ruling Class." Available at *The Atlantic Magazine* (January/February). Available at www.theatlantic.com/magazine/archive/2005/01/lost-in-the-meritocracy/3672/.

Lehrer, Jonah. 2011. "The Virtues of Play." *Wired* (March 16). Available at www.wired.com/wiredscience/2011/03/the-virtues-of-play/.

Murphy, James Bernard. 2011. "In Defense of Being a Kid." *The Wall Street Journal*, February 9. Available at http://online.wsj.com/article/SB10001424052748704709304576124612242184274.html.

Robinson, Ken. 2001. *Out of Our Minds: Learning to Be Creative.* West Sussex, UK: Capstone.

Robison, John Elder. 2011. *Be Different: Adventures of a Free-Range Aspergian with Practical Advice for Aspergians, Misfits, Families, and Teachers.* New York: Random House.

Sandburg, Carl. 2007. *Abraham Lincoln: The Prairie Years and the War Years.* New York: Sterling.

Sarason, Seymour. 2004. *And What Do YOU Mean by Learning?* Portsmouth, NH: Heinemann.

Sennett, Richard. 2008. *The Craftsman.* New Haven: Yale University Press.

Thackera, John. 2005. *In the Bubble: Designing in a Complex World.* Cambridge, MA: The MIT Press.

Thompson, Mark. 2011. Speech at Big Bang Australia.

White House, The. 2009. *Fact Sheet: No Child Left Behind Has Raised Expectations and Improved Results.* The White House, President George W. Bush. Available at http://georgewbush-whitehouse.archives.gov/infocus/education/. Accessed July 28, 2012.

# CHAPTER 3

Auden, W. H. [1938] n.d. "Musée des Beaux Arts." Retrieved from http://english.emory.edu/classes/paintings&poems/auden.html.

British Broadcasting Company (BBC). 2011. "Mark Zuckerberg: Inside Facebook." Interview by Emily Maitlis. London: BBC.

Caplan, Ralph. 2008. Conversation about leaving-to-learn programs, February 8.

Childress, Herb. 2000. *Landscapes of Betrayal, Landscapes of Joy: Curtisville in the Lives of Its Teenagers, SUNY Series in Environmental and Architectural Phenomenology.* New York: State University of New York Press.

Csikszentmihalyi, Mihaly. 1997. *Finding Flow: The Psychology of Engagement with Everyday Life*. New York: HarperCollins.

Harrington, Maureen. 2010. "Muse School Is Actress' Brainchild." *Los Angeles Times*, March 6. Available at http://articles.latimes.com/2010/mar/06/entertainment/la-et-muse6-2010mar06.

Martin, Roger L. 2009a. Electronic mail message, November 14.

———. 2009b. *The Design of Business: Why Design Thinking Is the Next Competitive Advantage*. Boston: Harvard Business School.

Nietzsche, Friedrich. [1882] 2009. *The Gay Science (The Joyful Wisdom)*. Translated by Thomas Common. New York: Random House.

Putnam, Robert D. 1995. "Bowling Alone: America's Declining Social Capital." *Journal of Democracy* 1. Available at http://muse.jhu.edu/login?auth=0&type=summary&url=/journals/journal_of_democracy/v006/6.1putnam.html.

Robison, John Elder. 2011. *Be Different: Adventures of a Free-Range Aspergian with Practical Advice for Aspergians, Misfits, Families, and Teachers*. New York: Random House.

Rothstein, Richard. 2001. "LESSONS; Weighing Students' Skills and Underlying Attitudes." *New York Times*, May 16. Available at www.nytimes.com/2001/05/16/nyregion/lessons-weighing-students-skills-and-underlying-attitudes.html.

# CHAPTER 4

Florida, Richard. 2005. *Cities and the Creative Class*. New York: Routledge.

Glaeser, Edward L. 2011. *Triumph of the City: How Our Greatest Invention Makes Us Richer, Smarter, Greener, Healthier, and Happier*. New York: Penguin.

Hopkins, Gerard Manley. [1877] 1963. *Poems and Prose, Penguin Classics*. New York: Penguin.

Mojkowski, Charles, and Elliot Washor. 2011. "What Employers Don't Know About Their New Hires, and Why." *Techniques* (October): 10–11.

Page, Scott E. 2007. *The Difference: How the Power of Diversity Creates Better Groups, Firms, Schools, and Societies*. Princeton: Princeton University Press.

Sarason, Seymour. 2004. *And What Do YOU Mean by Learning?* Portsmouth, NH: Heinemann.

Stevenson, Robert Louis. [1882] 2006. *Familiar Studies of Men and Books*. Charleston, SC: BiblioBazaar.

TED.com. 2006. "Ken Robinson Says Schools Kill Creativity," Filmed in February, posted in June 2006. Available at www.ted.com/talks/ken_robinson_says_schools_kill_creativity.html. Accessed July 28, 2012.

# Chapter 5

Anderson, Jenny. 2011. "From Finland, an Intriguing School-Reform Model." *New York Times*, December 12. Available at http://www.nytimes.com/2011/12/13/education/from-finland-an-intriguing-school-reform-model.html?pagewanted=all.

Austen, Hilary. 2010. *Artistry Unleashed: A Guide to Pursuing Great Performance in Work and Life.* Toronto, ON: University of Toronto Press.

Berger, Ron. 2003. *An Ethic of Excellence: Building a Culture of Craftsmanship with Students.* Portsmouth, NH: Heinemann.

Birks, J. B. 1962. *Rutherford at Manchester.* London: Heywood.

Drucker, P. F. 1995. *Managing in a Time of Great Change.* New York: Truman Talley Books.

Eisner, Elliot. 1985. *Learning and Teaching the Ways of Knowing.* Chicago: National Society for the Study of Education.

Gardner, Howard. 1999. *The Disciplined Mind: What All Students Should Understand.* New York: Simon & Schuster.

Gladwell, Malcolm. 2008. *Outliers: The Story of Success.* New York: Little, Brown.

Hancock, LynNell. 2011. "Why Are Finland's Schools Successful?" *Smithsonian* magazine, (September). Available at www.smithsonianmag.com/people-places/Why-Are-Finlands-Schools-Successful.html.

Lerman, Robert I., and Arnold Packer. 2010. "Will We Ever Learn? What's Wrong with the Common-Standards Project." *Education Week*, April 21. Available at www.urban.org/publications/901345.html.

Leski, Kyna. 2012. *Design Intelligences: Kyna Leski's Thoughts on Navigating the Creative Process.* Available at http://designintelligences.wordpress.com/. Accessed May 17, 2012.

Mrpotatohead.net. n.d. *Mr. Potato Head on TV and Movies.* Available at www.mrpotatohead.net/tv/tv.htm. Accessed March 13, 2012.

Robinson, Ken. 2001. *Out of Our Minds: Learning to Be Creative.* West Sussex, UK: Capstone.

Senge, Peter. 1990. *The Fifth Discipline: The Art and Practice of the Learning Organization, Innovation Associates.* New York: Doubleday.

Sennett, Richard. 2008. *The Craftsman.* New Haven: Yale University Press.

Walsh, Tim. 2005. *Timeless Toys: Classic Toys and the Playmakers Who Created Them.* Kansas City: Andrews McMeel.

Washor, Elliot, and Charles Mojkowski. 2005. "Standards and Variation: Nonconform-ing Our Way to High Quality." *Education Week*, September 14, 34–36.

———. 2006–2007. "What Do You Mean by Rigor?" *Educational Leadership* 64 (4): 84–87.

# Chapter 6

Bloom, Benjamin S. 1986. "Automaticity: The Hands and Feet of Genius." *Educational Leadership* 43 (5): 70–77.

Borte, Jason, and Surfline Editorial. 2012. *Sean Collins* (April 8, 1952–December 26, 2011). Surfline.com. Available at www.surfline.com/surfing-a-to-z/sean-collins-biography-and-photos_784/. Accessed January 25, 2012.

Brant, John. 2005. "What One Man Can Do." *Inc.* (September 1). Available at www.inc.com/magazine/20050901/bill-strickland_pagen_7.html.

Darling-Hammond, Linda. 2011. "Linda Darling-Hammond on Teacher Evaluations Through Student Testing." NBC News *Education Nation* blog, May 25. Available at www.educationnation.com/index.cfm?objectid=E730EFBA-86ED-11E0-B74E000C296BA163. Accessed August 5, 2012.

Dwyer, Aidan. 2011. *Aidan: The Secret of the Fibonacci Sequence in Trees*. Paper submitted for the 2011 Young Naturalist Award, American Museum of Natural History. Available at http://www.amnh.org/learn-teach/young-naturalist-awards/winners/2011/the-secret-of-the-fibonacci-sequence-in-trees. Accessed November 6, 2012.

Fairtest.org. 2007. *Multiple-Choice Tests*. The National Center for Fair and Open Testing, August 17. Available at www.fairtest.org/multiple-choice-tests. Accessed August 5, 2012.

Johnston, Joe, dir. 1999. *October Sky*. Produced by Universal Pictures.

Leski, Kyna. 2012. *Design Intelligences: Kyna Leski's Thoughts on Navigating the Creative Process*. Available from http://designintelligences.wordpress.com/. Accessed May 17, 2012.

Marsalis, Wynton. 2008. *Moving to Higher Ground: How Jazz Can Change Your Life*. New York: Random House.

Martin, Roger L. 2009. "The Science and Art of Business." *Rotman Magazine* (Winter): 4–8.

Noddings, Nel. 2005. *The Challenge to Care in Schools: An Alternative Approach to Education*. New York: Teachers College Press.

Page, Dan. 2001. "Nicholas Negroponte: Digital Visionary." *Converge* magazine 4 (10): 38–40, 49.

Sanders, Lisa. 2009. *Every Patient Tells a Story: Medical Mysteries and the Art of Diagnosis*. New York: Broadway.

Washor, Elliot, and Charles Mojkowski. 2011a. "The Knowledge Funnel: A New Model for Learning" (Part 1 of 2). *Edutopia*, April 5. Available at http://www.edutopia.org/blog/knowledge-funnel-learning-elliot-washor-charles-mojkowski. Accessed August 5, 2012.

———. 2011b. "Use the Learning Funnel to Design Meaningful Work for Students" (Part 2 of 2). *Edutopia*, April 4. Available at www.edutopia.org/blog/learning-funnel-design-meaningful-work-elliot-washor-charles-mojkowski. Accessed August 5, 2012.

# Chapter 7

Caplan, R. 2008. Personal communication about leaving-to-learn programs with Elliot Washor, February 8.

Fong, D. 2012. "Beaverton Teacher to Be Recognized for Starting Farm at Terra Nova High School." Oregonlive.com, March 28. Available at www.oregonlive.com/beaverton/index.ssf/2012/03/beaverton_teacher_to_be_recogn.html.

Gardner, H., M. Csikszentmihalyi, and W. Damon. 2001. *Good Work: When Excellence and Ethics Meet*. New York: Basic Books.

Goetz, K. 2011. "How 3M Gave Everyone Days Off and Created an Innovation Dynamo." *Fast Co.Design*, www.fastcodesign.com/1663137/how-3m-gave-everyone-days-off-and-created-an-innovation-dynamo.

Makerspace. 2012. "What Is Makerspace?" Available at http://makerspace.com/about/. Accessed August 9, 2012.

Mediratta, B., and J. Bick. 2007. "The Google Way: Give Engineers Room." *New York Times*, October 21. Available at www.nytimes.com/2007/10/21/jobs/21pre.html.

Richardson, C. 2011. "It's His Golden Opportunity: New Leader's Plan to Revive Palace Cathedral." *New York Daily News*, September 22. Available at www.nydailynews.com/new-york/uptown/golden-opportunity-new-leader-plan-revive-palace-cathedral-article-1.954521.

Rose, M. 2004. *The Mind at Work: Valuing the Intelligence of the American Worker*. New York: Viking.

Sanchez, E. 2012. Email communication to Elliot Washor, July 10.

Sito, T. 2008. "The Prism: A Profile of Dave Master." *Animation World Network*, May 20. Available at www.awn.com/articles/profiles/prism-profile-dave-master/page/2,1. Accessed August 9, 2012.

Wisdom Series, The. 2010. *The Wisdom of George Santayana*. New York: Open Road.

Wooden, J., and S. Jamison. 1997. *Wooden: A Lifetime of Observations and Reflections On and Off the Court*. Chicago: Contemporary Books.

# Chapter 8

Bennis, W. G., and R. J. Thomas. 2002. *Geeks and Geezers: How Era, Values, and Defining Moments Shape Leaders*. Boston: Harvard Business School.

Carson, R. L., and N. Kelsh. 1956. *The Sense of Wonder.* New York: HarperCollins.

Oldenburg, R. 1989. *The Great Good Place: Cafes, Coffee Shops, Bookstores, Bars, Hair Salons, and Other Hangouts at the Heart of a Community.* New York: Marlowe.

Washor, E., C. Mojkowski, and L. Newsom. 2009. "At the Core of the Apple Store: Images of Next Generation Learning." *Phi Delta Kappan* 91: 60–63.

## CHAPTER 9

Christensen, C. M., S. D. Anthony, G. Berstell, and D. Nitterhouse. 2007. "Finding the Right Job for Your Product." *MIT Sloan Management Review* 48 (3): 38–47.

Hamel, G. 1996. "Strategy as Revolution." *Harvard Business Review* 74 (4): 69–82.

Morgan, E., E. Olsson, and S. Traill. 2012. *Learn Anytime, Anywhere: Rethinking How Students Earn Credit Beyond School Hours.* New York: The After-School Corporation (TASC).

Postman, N. 1982. *The Disappearance of Childhood.* New York: Delacorte.

Reed, C., dir. 1949. *The Third Man.* Produced by C. Reed, A. Korda and D. Selznick, United Kingdom.

## CHAPTER 10

Caplan, R. 2005. *By Design: Why There Are No Locks on the Bathroom Doors in the Hotel Louis XIV and Other Object Lessons.* New York: Fairchild Books.

Christensen, C. M. 1997. *The Innovator's Dilemma: The Revolutionary Book That Will Change the Way You Do Business.* Boston: Harvard Business School.

Goodwin, J. S., and J. M. Goodwin. 1984. "The Tomato Effect: Rejection of Highly Efficacious Therapies." *JAMA* 251 (18): 2387–90.

Hague, U. 2011. *Betterness: Economics for Humans.* Boston: Harvard Business Review.

Isaacson, W. 2011. *Steve Jobs.* New York: Simon & Schuster.

Lahr, J. 2005. "Sweet and Sour: Elaine May and Julia Cho Dish up Despair." *The New Yorker*, June 13. Available at www.newyorker.com/archive/2005/06/13/050613crth_theatre.

Malcolm, J. 1997. *In the Freud Archives.* New York: The New York Review of Books.

Sarason, S. 2004. *And What Do YOU Mean by Learning?* Portsmouth, NH: Heinemann.

Segen's Medical Dictionary. 2012. "Tomato Effect." Available at http://medical-dictionary.thefreedictionary.com/Tomato+Effect. Accessed May 11, 2012.

TED.com. 2010. "Charles Leadbeater: Education Innovation in the Slums." Filmed in April, posted in June. Available at www.ted.com/talks/charles_leadbeater_on_education.html. Accessed May 14, 2012.

Thiel Foundation. 2011. "Thiel Fellowship." January 23. Available at www.thielfellowship.org/. Accessed January 23, 2012.

Turkle, S. 2005. *The Second Self: Computers and the Human Spirit.* 20th anniversary ed. Cambridge, MA: The MIT Press.

Wilson, F. 2012. Electronic message to Elliot Washor, February 18.

You can follow the authors' ongoing work on leaving-to-learn programs and practices at **www. leavingtolearn.org**.

## ELLIOT WASHOR

Elliot Washor cofounded and codirects Big Picture Learning. Involved in school reform for more than 35 years as a teacher, principal, writer, and speaker, Elliot has worked all over the world designing and developing innovative schools that provide engaging learning environments for students and adults. Elliot's interests lie in how schools connect with communities to credit learning that occurs both in and outside of school. The George Lucas Foundation has selected Elliot as one of The Daring Dozen—The Twelve Most Daring Educators.

Elliot lives in sunny San Diego with his wife and their Portuguese Podengo Pequenos. You can e-mail Elliot at ewashor@gmail.com.

## CHARLES MOJKOWSKI

Charles Mojkowski has worked as a consultant to education and business organizations for more than 35 years. He works primarily in the areas of school, program, and curriculum design; leadership and organizational development; and innovative applications of technology in these areas. He has authored numerous articles on unconventional designs for schools and schooling.

He is a former English teacher, elementary school assistant principal, and administrator in the Rhode Island Department of Education. He was also an associate professor in the doctoral program in Educational Leadership at Johnson & Wales University.

He lives in Cranston, Rhode Island, with Corinne, his wife of 45 years.